SEEK
AND YOU WILL
FIND

DISCOVERING A
PRACTICE OF PRAYER

RHONDA MAWHOOD LEE

Library of Congress Cataloging-in-Publication Data

Names: Lee, Rhonda Mawhood, 1966- author.
Title: Seek and you will find : discovering a practice of prayer / Rhonda
    Mawhood Lee.
Description: Cincinnati, Ohio : Forward Movement, [2021] | Includes
    bibliographical references. | Summary: "Prayer is a primary way
    Christians fulfill the Great Commandment to love God, our neighbor, and
    ourselves, and it's the foundation of everything else we do to show that
    love. In prayer, we consciously devote time to cultivating our
    relationship with God, trusting that this relationship can transform our
    souls, our lives, and the world. Many of us who desire this closer
    relationship with God may feel unsure about where to start and how to
    pray. In Seek and You Will Find, Rhonda Mawhood Lee explores practices
    from the Lord's Prayer to praying with the psalms and in song, from the
    eucharist and the rosary to "moving" prayers offered when walking a
    labyrinth, doodling, baking, or devoting another activity to God.
    Scripture and tradition show us that when we seek God through prayer, we
    will find, by grace, the One who has already reached out to us in love.
    Seek and You Will Find is a comforting, challenging, and instructive
    companion in your quest to develop the relationship God deeply desires
    with you"-- Provided by publisher.
Identifiers: LCCN 2021019927 (print) | LCCN 2021019928 (ebook) | ISBN
    9780880284974 | ISBN 9780880284974 (ebook)
Subjects: LCSH: Prayer--Christianity.
Classification: LCC BV215 .L375 2021 (print) | LCC BV215 (ebook) | DDC
    248.3/2--dc23
LC record available at https://lccn.loc.gov/2021019927
LC ebook record available at https://lccn.loc.gov/2021019928

© 2021 Forward Movement
All rights reserved.
ISBN: 978-0-88028-497-4
Printed in USA

www.forwardmovement.org

SEEK
AND YOU WILL
FIND

DISCOVERING A
PRACTICE OF PRAYER

RHONDA MAWHOOD LEE

Forward Movement
Cincinnati, Ohio

Dedication

For friends who taught me to pray
and who persisted in prayer for and with me:

Angela

Donna

Joanna, fcJ

Lauren

Michael, Michael, and Michael (you know who you are)

Sarah

Table of Contents

Introduction

How do you pray?

I don't mean, how does one pray, or how should, or might, some hypothetical Christian pray.

I mean, how do *you* pray?

If you're like many disciples of Jesus, you may think you don't pray enough. You may fear you're not doing it right. You may not know where to start. You may wonder what "counts" as prayer, whether you need to use words, and if so, which words to use.

There may not be anyone with whom you feel comfortable speaking these questions and doubts out loud.

And at the root of all these questions might lie a deeper one, even more challenging to name: how can I, just a regular person, a sinner by definition, approach God, who is all-knowing, all-seeing, and perfect?

Our spiritual ancestors wrestled with the same question, and they answered it through stories.

The third chapter of the book of Genesis contains one of those stories, an account of the first moment of human self-consciousness. To many, the narrative is familiar: after Adam and Eve eat the fruit of the tree of the knowledge of good and evil, they realize they're naked, and they sew themselves fig-leaf loincloths. Even after they've covered up, the sound of God their Creator "walking in the garden at the time of the evening breeze" sends them into hiding.

Instead of just strolling on by, God seeks them out, calling, "Where are you?"

Through the ensuing conversation with God, human beings realize their single act of taking and eating has changed them forever. They know things now that they didn't before, and that other animals do not. They know they are naked and that they will die one day. They know they are free to do as God tells them—or not. They know that they will find it easier to blame others for deeds they regret than to take responsibility themselves—Adam points to Eve, who faults the serpent. And they know, now, that the consequences of their actions will not only affect themselves but will also reverberate through their family tree. From now on, Eden will be a lost ancestral land, for which their descendants will long.

Even as they gain all of these disturbing, even painful, new insights, Adam and Eve see that their actions haven't destroyed their Creator's love for them. God's final act before the couple leaves Eden is to hand-sew the clothing that will protect them in their new life.

Perhaps the most important thing Adam and Eve know, as they depart, is that even when shame drives them to slink behind the nearest tree, God will seek them out. The all-knowing, all-seeing God who brought them into being and sustains their every breath asks questions like, "Where are you?" "Who told you that you were naked?" and "What is this that you have done?" Even though God (presumably) already knows the answers to these queries, their Creator wants to stay in conversation with them, and by giving an account of their actions, they might learn to understand themselves better. More accurately, God wants to *start* that conversation with them. God is always interested, always ready to listen, even before we're ready to speak.

Adam and Eve's conversation with God, who asks, "Where are you?", is humanity's first prayer.

The first human beings may have discovered that prayer begins when we stand exposed before God, but virtually every person since then has resisted that insight. One of my favorite stories about prayer, told to me by my friend, the late United Methodist pastor Vernon C. Tyson, encapsulates our resistance.

An elderly widow shared with him a regret that had gnawed at her since her husband of nearly sixty years had died: that she had never loved him as well as he had deserved. When Vernon pointed out that she had always appeared to be a devoted wife, she poured out the story she had kept locked up for decades. In her late teens, she had fallen madly in love with Billy, the handsome, witty boy of her dreams and a great dancer, too. But he left her for another girl, and by the time he came to his senses and begged forgiveness, it was too late. She was already engaged to the old friend who had swooped in to woo her away from the man he believed had never deserved her. They committed to a life together; Billy moved away, and she and Billy never spoke again.

But from time to time over the years, she had thought of her first love. Now, with her husband gone and her own mortality looming, she worried. Had he realized she sometimes reminisced about Billy? Even if he hadn't, had the regret she felt over losing her first love infected her marriage, holding her back from showing her husband the affection he deserved?

Vernon gently reassured her: she and her husband had built a life on shared interests, raised kind children together, and enjoyed their time as empty-nesters. The smiles Vernon had seen on her husband's face as he looked at her had told their pastor everything he needed to know about the state of their marriage. And, he admonished the widow, she shouldn't forget how lovingly she had nursed her husband in his final months.

The lady's hesitant smile acknowledged Vernon might be right. When he said, "Why don't we pray?" she bowed her head. She relaxed as her pastor thanked God for long life, for the gift of marriage and children, for the shared joys and companionship that had seen her and her husband through hard times. "And, Lord," he added, "we thank you for the fervor of youth, for the gift of romance, and for a boy named Billy."

With that, his parishioner's head snapped up, her eyes flew open, and she gasped, "Reverend Tyson! Don't tell God *that*!"

At times, I have been that elderly widow, and I suspect you may have too. But the bedrock assumption of Christian prayer, affirmed by scripture and tradition dating back before the origins of the church, is that we have nothing to fear by standing naked before God. When we cry out to God, we respond to the One who has already reached out to us. God has already initiated our conversation because our Creator wants to be in relationship with us. Even though God already knows each of us better than we will ever know ourselves, God delights in us so deeply that the overwhelming divine desire is to keep company with us. Rashi, the medieval French rabbi, makes this point. Walking in Eden's pleasant evening breeze, God knew perfectly well where Adam was, Rashi says. Still, God asked, "Where are you?" Rashi contends God "asked this in order to enter into language with him."[1] Even knowing that humanity had already begun to separate from the easy union between Creator and beloved creatures, God wanted to start a conversation with human beings.

Time devoted to being consciously in the presence of God, speaking and listening, and also in companionable silence is prayer. It's time that deepens our relationship with God: the kind of time we devote to friends, family, lovers, spouses; time passed talking, revealing ourselves, and also listening, getting to know the other, growing ever closer; time that shapes us into better friends of God, better neighbors to each other, and ultimately better nurturers of ourselves too. Prayer is one way in which we fulfill the Great Commandment to love God, our neighbor, and ourselves, and it's the foundation of everything else we do to show that love.

For something so integral to the practice of our faith, prayer remains stubbornly mysterious. You and I have questions about prayer as old as Christianity itself: What happens when we pray? Do our prayers change anything? How should we pray?

Most obviously, we pray because Jesus did, and he told his disciples to do so as well. The gospels tell us that, along with participating in sabbath prayers in synagogues and praying in front of the crowds gathered around him, Jesus frequently went off to commune alone with God. He encouraged his friends to pray for the things they needed and even for things they wanted. When needing guidance, they asked him, "Lord, teach us to pray," he obliged, offering what Christians call the Lord's Prayer. And he went further, encouraging his friends to speak boldly to God who seeks us out with the determination of a shepherd going after an errant sheep or a woman sweeping until her lost coin glitters among the gathered dust, who loves us even more deeply than the most nurturing parent. "Ask," Jesus said, "and it will be given to you; seek, and you will find; knock, and the door will be opened to you. For everyone who asks receives, the one who seeks finds, and to the one who knocks, the door will be opened. Which of you, if your son asks for bread, will give him a stone? Or if he asks for a fish, will give him a snake? If you, then, though you are evil, know how to give good gifts to your children, how much more will your Father in heaven give good gifts to those who ask him!"[2]

If I had been in the crowd gathered around Jesus the day he offered that reassurance, I imagine I would have felt both relieved to know that God wanted me to voice my needs and desires and also skeptical.

Would I have been brave enough to voice my skepticism? To say, "Jesus, I have worked as an advocate for child survivors of sexual abuse and child witnesses to domestic violence. I have known infants who no longer cried because they had already learned it was useless—no one would answer, and I have met parents who justified child abuse as acts of love. I have prayed for all those children and parents, and I don't know if my prayers ever did any good."

These questions about whether our prayers make a difference didn't originate with me. In the fifth century, Saint Augustine of Hippo responded to Proba, a widow who had written him about prayer, that Christians ought to feel "desolate": conscious of our separation from God, conscious of the distance between our lives and what God desires for us. That sense of desolation, itself, should lead us to "continue in prayer, and learn to fix the eye of faith on the word of the divine scriptures as 'on a light shining in a dark place until the dawn, and the day-star arise in our hearts.'"[3] Centuries later, Thomas Aquinas laid out three effects of prayer. First, the merit of the act (it is, itself, a good thing for Christians to do); second, what he called "impetration," or beseeching God to give us the good things God indeed wants to provide; and third, "the spiritual refreshment of the mind."[4] As we beseech God to provide good things—for the abused children I worked with, among others—we may also become aware of the ways in which we can align ourselves with God's actions by sharing what we have with our neighbors. In Aquinas's words, our actions can align us with God's purposes in the same way that time set apart for prayer can: "As long as a person is acting in their heart, speech, or work in such a manner that they are tending toward God, they are praying; and thus one who is directing their whole life toward God is praying always."[5]

Ideally, if we are listening for God and to God, our desires will, although perhaps at a glacial pace, become aligned with God's desires for us and our neighbors. In other words, by grace, we may eventually stop praying for those things we don't truly need or even, in the deepest reaches of ourselves, really want. By grace, as we pray for our neighbors who are suffering, we may be moved to offer them something of what they need—whether emotional, spiritual, or material—out of the good things God has given us. Fourteenth-century English mystic Julian of Norwich, who lived through the devastation of the plague and offered hope to a traumatized generation, wrote, "Prayer unites the soul to God." By God's own grace, prayer shrinks the gap that sin carves between humanity and divinity. God teaches us to pray and to trust we will receive what we request, "for," as Julian said, "he beholds us in love, and wants to make us partners in his good will and work….Therefore we pray to him urgently that he may do what is pleasing to him, as if he were to say: How could you please me more than by entreating me, urgently, wisely, and sincerely, to do the thing that I want to have done? And so the soul by prayer is made of one accord with God."[6]

Like our forebears all the way back to humanity's first moment of consciousness, you and I pray as sinners in a world marked by sin, death, epic tragedies, and mundane disappointments. Innocent children die while tyrants live into their nineties. Hurricanes and earthquakes devastate nations already plundered by colonial powers and the legacy of enslavement. That all this transpires despite fervent prayer is a sorrowful mystery that, it seems, won't be resolved this side of eternal life.

And yet Christians trust that we pray also as beloved children of God in a world transformed by the life, death, and resurrection of Jesus; in a world shaped by the power of the Holy Spirit, who moves within us. Jesus offers us a faith rooted in an empty tomb and shapes us into a community within which we are called to, in Paul's words, "rejoice with those who rejoice, weep with those who weep" (Romans 12:15). The Lord who taught his friends to pray also offered an implicit rebuke when they were unable to exorcise a particularly stubborn demon that, in the end, Jesus himself had to deal with. When his disciples asked, "Why could we not cast it out?" Jesus explained, "This kind can come out only through prayer" (Mark 9:29). By prayer, he seemed to mean the unity with God that he embodied and that Christians like Julian have suggested is possible for us, too.

Jesus's assessment of his friends' work has implications for his disciples today. If demons—the body-crushing, soul-sucking forces of death that wear many disguises—still romp their way through God's redeemed creation, the gospels seem to suggest this is true not only because we live in a fallen world but also because we Christians have not fully tapped the power that lies within us, as the Body of Christ. Through prayer, we align ourselves with that power.

How, then, shall we pray?

You may have heard it said, or you may yourself have said, "I can pray anywhere, doing anything. My work is my prayer; watching my children play is prayer; doing yoga or walking in the woods is prayer." And in a sense, any time passed consciously in God's presence can be a form of prayer.

But our relationship with God, like all our relationships, needs to have time specifically devoted to it to flourish. Time in which you reveal yourself; time in which you listen, pay attention to the other. Time to appreciate the long-established patterns of the relationship, and time enough to be surprised, too, by learning new things about the other or the insights about yourself they reflect back to you. Teresa of Ávila, a sixteenth-century mystic, writer, and founder of the Discalced Carmelite Order, offered reassurance to her sisters who were nervous about approaching God, hesitant to engage the Creator, Redeemer, and Sustainer of the universe as one would a friend. She said that God "will inspire you with what to say," and asked, "Since you speak with other persons, why must words fail you more when you speak with God?"[7] Like Teresa's nuns, most of us need help to learn how to approach God and cultivate our relationship.

Over the past two thousand years, Christians have developed techniques and practices of prayer to help devote time to their friendship with God and, by grace, to grow as a result.

I wrote this book to help you learn and practice some of those forms of prayer. In the chapters that follow, I reflect on a variety of different prayers or practices:

the Lord's Prayer

Holy Eucharist (variously called the Mass, Holy Communion, and the Lord's Supper)

the Daily Office (sets of prayers prescribed for various times of the day)

praying with the psalms

the rosary

the intercession of the saints

Ignatian prayer (imaginative prayer, the examen, and the Spiritual Exercises, practices developed by Saint Ignatius of Loyola, the founder of the Society of Jesus)

Lectio Divina

praying through song

movement prayers

silent prayers

working with a spiritual director

Woven into these practices are some or all of the various types of Christian prayer:

adoration (placing oneself consciously in the presence of God, or more aptly, remembering that one is already there, for the sheer pleasure of keeping company with God)

praise (glorifying God for who God is)

thanksgiving (for what God has done for us and/or for others)

penitence (confessing our sins)

oblation (offering our lives and labors to God)

intercession (asking for good things for other people)

petition (asking for good things for ourselves)[8]

In these reflections, I offer glimpses of my own prayer life as an Episcopal priest, a spiritual director in the tradition of Saint Ignatius, and one whose own spiritual nurturer of many years is a member of the Society of Friends (also called Quakers). In my prayer, work, and play, I seek to be what the Jesuits (members of Ignatius's Society of Jesus) call "a contemplative in action": a Christian who pauses, reflects, and then resumes activity before pausing and reflecting again. By grace and over time, this cycle helps me better to appreciate and accept God's love for me and also helps me better show love to my fellow creatures of God. Habitual prayer becomes the basis for faithful action.

My approach to prayer is inevitably shaped by the fact that I am a North American of European origin, a respectfully (I hope) appreciative student and observer of cultures that are not my own, and yet limited in my perspective as everyone is. I hope this book may be a springboard to those readers who may turn elsewhere to learn more about, for example, First Nations' adaptations of Anglican daily prayers or the charismatic, ecstatic experiences of prayer often associated with the Pentecostal tradition.

Throughout this book, I share some of my joys, offer some confessions, and possibly even bear witness to the occasional miracle. All this comes with an invitation for you to learn and explore the various types of prayers and, ultimately, to discover your own practice of prayer. As you try the various forms of prayer offered in these pages, please be gentle with yourself. Consistent practice of prayer typically offers benefits, but people often feel self-conscious when adopting a new form of prayer. It's also common to experience periodic "dry spells" in our relationship with God. You may find it easier to notice patterns in your practice and gain insight into your relationship with God and your neighbor if you keep a prayer journal, whether in a bound book, on a computer, through a notes app on your phone or in the margins of this book, by sketching, or in any other way that allows you to store your observations and return to them later. Talking with a friend, prayer group, or spiritual director can be helpful too. And remember, temperament plays a role in our prayer, just as it does in other areas of life. Some of these practices may stick with you for a lifetime or only for a season. Some may never resonate with you at all. This book is simply an invitation to you to try on any or all of them to see how they might fit.

It is my hope that you won't journey through these pages alone. Even though many forms of prayer can be practiced alone, Christian prayer is fundamentally a community endeavor. The prayer Jesus taught his disciples opens with "Our Father" for a reason. A devout Jew, Jesus was raised in a faith that prioritized corporate prayer. Even though he went off to pray by himself from time to time and encouraged his followers to do the same, he always returned to the group. After his resurrection and ascension, his disciples regularly gathered to pray. The two foundational sacraments of the church, baptism and eucharist, explicitly bring us into Jesus Christ's Body and then nourish us as members of that Body. Even when we pray alone, we're still connected at a mystical level with the Body's other members, in this life and the next.

To help you and your companions along the way, I offer guidelines at the end of each chapter about how to start practicing each form of prayer and questions to help you reflect on those experiences. As you use this book, I pray that you will come to know yourself better as God's beloved, and I pray you will also grow closer to siblings in Christ as you seek, together, to deepen your friendship with God who delights in us all and is already calling us to draw closer.

Endnotes

[1] Discussed in Avivah Gottlieb Zornberg, *The Murmuring Deep: Reflections on the Biblical Unconscious* (New York: Knopf Doubleday, 2009), 19. Thanks to Lauren F. Winner for the reference.

[2] Matthew 7:7-11, New International Version.

[3] Augustine, Letter 130, quoting 2 Peter 1:19, http://www.newadvent.org/fathers/1102130.htm, accessed 29 February 2020.

[4] Thomas Aquinas, *Summa Theologiae* 83:13, http://www.newadvent.org/summa/3083.htm#article13, accessed 29 February 2020.

[5] Cited in Ignatius of Loyola, *Spiritual Exercises and Selected Works,* trans. George E. Ganss, sj (Mahwah, NJ: Paulist Press, 1991), 459 (gender-neutral language mine).

[6] Julian of Norwich, *Showings,* trans. James Walsh, sj, and ed. Edmund Colledge, osa, (Mahwah, NJ: Paulist Press, 1978), 253-254.

[7] Teresa of Ávila, "The Way of Perfection," 27:9, in *The Collected Works, Vol. Two,* trans. Kieran Kavanaugh, ocd, and Otilio Rodríguez (Washington, D.C.: Institute of Carmelite Studies, 1980).

[8] Various typologies of Christian prayer exist. Here I follow the one given in the Catechism of the Book of Common Prayer 1979 of the Episcopal Church, 856; https://bcponline.org/.

The Lord's Prayer

That Sunday morning in Bethlehem's Christmas Lutheran Church, I hadn't understood a word of the scripture readings or Pastor Mitri Raheb's homily. I hadn't expected to. A dozen fellow seminarians and I had signed up for this intensive course, led by our Hebrew professor, to visit Israel and the West Bank and get to know their people. A sense of dislocation was part of the package deal. We holders of North American passports sailed through checkpoints where Palestinians waited for hours in the sun on the off chance they might be admitted to Israel to work that day. We listened to the frustrations and dreams of people from all ethnic backgrounds and political persuasions, people who could meet with us but not with each other because of the Israeli government's travel restrictions. And we snapped digital photographs of each other beside the 10,000-year-old walls of Jericho and the house at Capernaum that may well have belonged to the Apostle Peter's mother.

In Pastor Mitri's church, I felt a little more at home. When he stood behind the altar and lifted the bread, he uttered one of the few Arabic words I knew—*layla*, night. I realized he was repeating the story Christians have told since our earliest days, the story Paul repeated in his first letter to the church in Corinth, which we have come to call the "words of institution" of the eucharist. "The Lord Jesus on the night he was betrayed took bread…In the same way he took the cup also…"

But it was after Pastor Mitri had lifted the consecrated bread and broken it that our visiting group truly found our place in the liturgy. After lowering the bread and keeping a moment of silence, he began to speak again, and the congregation joined in. I couldn't understand a word, but the rhythm was so familiar that I began to pray too, in English. "Our Father in heaven…" One by one, all the way along our pew, we visitors linked hands and offered the words Jesus Christ himself taught us.

The Lord's Prayer, often called the Our Father, is the prayer millions of Christians around the world recite every day—and millions more turn to in stressful moments. We repeat it at virtually every worship service; we teach it to our children. In whatever language we offer the prayer, we make Jesus's original Aramaic words our own. If prayer is conversation with God, Jesus gave us an icebreaker.

Christians have been using this icebreaker since the earliest days of what was first called the Way, which we now call the church (the community of shared practice and mutual care that helps each other follow Jesus). *The Didache*, a first-century manual of how to live together as Christians, instructs Christians to offer the prayer three times a day (*Didache* means "training," as in the teaching a master artisan would give an apprentice).[1] Third- and fourth-century bishops like Saint Cyprian of Carthage and Saint Augustine of Hippo offered instruction to the faithful on how and why to pray the Lord's Prayer, and the earliest monastic rules assume monks and nuns will do so several times a day.

Not only does the Lord's Prayer come to us from the gospels (of Matthew and Luke, to be precise), but second-century North African writer Tertullian called it "the epitome of the whole Gospel."[2] Former Archbishop of Canterbury Rowan Williams echoed Tertullian by saying, "If somebody said, give me a summary of Christian faith on the back of an envelope, the best thing to do would be to write Our Lord's Prayer."[3] In Matthew's Gospel, the prayer appears as one part of what we call the Sermon on the Mount, Jesus's long series of lessons about what a life devoted to loving God and one's neighbor looks like. Amidst his teachings about how to pray, fast, give alms, and forgive, Jesus warns against "heap[ing] up empty phrases." Instead, he offers a simple series of affirmations and petitions:

> Our Father in heaven,
> > hallowed be your name.
> > Your kingdom come.
> > Your will be done,
> > > on earth as it is in heaven.
> > Give us this day our daily bread.
> > And forgive us our debts,
> > > as we also have forgiven our debtors.
> > And do not bring us to the time of trial,
> > > but rescue us from the evil one.[4]

The Lord's Prayer does two things: glorify God and ask that our physical and spiritual needs be met. Although the prayer is uniquely precious to Christians, it is deeply rooted in Jesus's Jewish tradition.[5] Contrary to some Christian claims, Jesus was not the first to call God Father. "I will be a father to him," the Lord promised David, speaking of the future King Solomon; centuries later, the prophet Malachi asked his people, "Have we not all one father? Has not one God created us?"[6]

Beyond his familiarity with the concept of God as Father, Jesus was raised on scriptural texts exalting God, like the command found in Leviticus 22:32, "You shall not profane my holy name, that I may be sanctified among the people of Israel: I am the LORD," and the human affirmation in Psalm 113, "Let the name of the LORD be blessed, from this time forth for evermore. From the rising of the sun to its going down let the name of the LORD be praised." And the sense that God is ever-present, caring for God's children even when they feel cut off from their divine Parent, permeates prophetic books like Isaiah: "Can a woman forget her nursing child, or show no compassion for the child of her womb? Even these may forget, yet I will not forget you."[7] For Christians, the words "Our Father" remind us that the Son prays with us and that we are kin to everyone who calls on the one, living God as Jesus did.

The prayer's opening words also have what New Testament scholar Amy-Jill Levine calls "a political edge." Jesus lived his life as a member of a nation ruled over by the Roman Emperor; his homeland was occupied by Caesar's army. Caesar was commonly called "father" to signify his authority over his subjects and their supposed child-like dependence on him. But for Jesus, a faithful Jew, Caesar has no monopoly on his subjects' loyalty nor is he the highest authority over them. "By speaking of the 'Father in heaven,'" Levine notes, "Jesus thus insists that Rome is not the 'true' father."[8] Twenty-first-century people need a reminder of history to catch this nuance of meaning, but it would have been clear to Jesus's first-century audience—Jews, Gentiles, and Roman occupiers alike.

Christians of different times and places have reminded themselves and each other of the political implications of addressing God as "Our Father." One example is Muriel Lester, an English peace activist and associate of Mahatma Gandhi. Gandhi was a leader of the Indian campaign for liberation from British rule and a strong influence on Martin Luther King Jr. and others committed to the African-American freedom struggle. Just before the Second World War, Lester wrote of the world's need for people who would struggle non-violently for justice: "Unless God meant the human race to be actually one family, we have no right to the phrase 'Our Father.' Unless Jesus was misinterpreting God, we cannot overcome evil with evil, or gain security by armies and navies, or defend ourselves by preparing to kill potential enemies."[9] The Lord's Prayer can both comfort and convict us as we pray for God's help to live as Jesus's friends.

When we're too tired or frightened to compose our own prayers, when we're not sure we can trust our own desires enough to voice them to God, or when we want to join other Christians in a prayer that crosses denominational divisions, the Lord's Prayer gives us words to express what we need. This has long been true. Drawing on his study of Augustine's writings, the medieval scholar Thomas Aquinas wrote that in the Lord's Prayer, "not only do we ask for all that we may rightly desire, but also in the order wherein we ought to desire them, so that this prayer not only teaches us to ask, but also directs all our affections." We start by glorifying God, implicitly asking to participate more fully in God's life. The divine name is already holy, and yet we pray that people might treat it as holy; God already reigns, and yet we pray that God's will might be perfectly done and that God might equip us to do it here and now. And then we move on to asking God to meet our needs: to feed us, both physically with enough food for today and also with a foretaste of the heavenly banquet through the eucharist; to forgive us; to keep us from trials we fear may undo us, as Jesus himself prayed on the night of his arrest, "My Father, if it is possible, let this cup pass from me"; and to rescue us from evil, whether the evil comes from outside ourselves or inside.[10] And we pray all these things knowing—or at least, trying to trust—that God desires our well-being not only in this life but in the age to come.

All of that is a lot for one prayer to contain. And yet, it's all there within the prayer Jesus left us as part of our inheritance from him.

At times, each of us may find some of the prayer's petitions harder to voice than others. Might "hallowed be your name" evoke a needle of shame at having yelled a few choice words in a fit of anger? If we're used to having enough to eat, do we glide over "Give us today our daily bread" as if we weren't dependent on God for our sustenance? Do we consider what we could do to ensure at least one neighbor also has what they need? When we hear "Forgive us our sins, as we forgive those who sin against us," are we spurred to be more forgiving, or are we unduly hard on ourselves, forgetting all the times we have, in fact, forgiven hurts both deep and trifling? Do we pray for people who are being harmed in ways that may make forgiveness challenging and reconciliation well-nigh impossible (in this life, anyway), and ask God for the ability to assist them in respectful ways? Do we support efforts to limit the harm human beings can inflict on each other? When offered thoughtfully and honestly, the Lord's Prayer can serve as a call to confession, a spur to amend our lives, and a channel of God's gracious power to aid us in revealing more of the divine reign on earth.

A complete prayer in itself, the Our Father is also a model for our personal prayers. Start by praising God, pray for God's will to be done, and then ask for what you need and want, even if you're afraid you might not get those things or won't receive them in the time frame you had in mind. Be as simple and direct as you can while knowing that God has all the time in the world— and boundless love—with which to listen. As you offer these prayers in your own words, you'll be following the example Jesus set, and you'll be learning what he teaches.

Questions to consider and things to try

✠ Notice where the Lord's Prayer comes up in corporate prayers, like in the eucharist. Does praying it in a group feel different from praying it on your own? Reflect on the differences and see what insights may follow your observations.

✠ Pray the Lord's Prayer once through, and then again more slowly, pausing over each petition. Notice the words that catch your attention, and consider what God may be saying to you through them.

> *Alternatively, pause after each petition to consider its specific meaning for you now. For example, as you pray, "Hallowed be your name," consider: for what, specifically, do you praise God in this moment? "Your will be done": what is one way in which you long to see God's will done? Offer those prayers.*

✠ If you normally worship in your native language, try learning the Lord's Prayer in a different language, perhaps one common among immigrants where you live or a language your ancestors may have spoken. How does praying these well-known words in an unfamiliar tongue affect your experience of the moment?

✠ Write a prayer modeled on the Our Father, addressing and praising God in your own words and offering your own petitions for yourself and others.

Endnotes

Aaron Milavec, *The Didache: Text, Translation, Analysis, and Commentary* (Collegeville, MN: Liturgical Press, 2003), 8:3.

[2] Tertullian, "On Prayer," Chapter 1, http://www.newadvent.org/fathers/0322.htm, accessed 21 March 2020.

[3] https://www.bbc.co.uk/religion/religions/christianity/prayer/lordsprayer_1.shtml, accessed 10 April 2020; Archbishop Rowan Williams and Sister Wendy Beckett, *Living the Lord's Prayer* (Oxford: Lion UK, 2008).

[4] Matthew 6:9-13. Translations of the prayer have varied somewhat over time, but Matthew's version, rather than Luke's virtually identical but shorter prayer (which you can find in his gospel at 11:2-4), is the one familiar to most Christians. In different versions of the prayer, "debts" might be rendered "trespasses" or "sins." The doxology with which many Christians conclude the prayer ("For the kingdom and the power and the glory are yours...") was added in the first century, appearing, for example, in *The Didache*.

[5] Amy-Jill Levine and Mark Zvi Brettler, eds., *The Jewish Annotated New Testament, 2nd ed.* (New York: Oxford University Press, 2017) offers this background on the Lord's Prayer and is a helpful corrective to harmful myths about the relationship between Judaism and Christianity.

[6] 2 Samuel 7:14, 1 Chronicles 22:9-10, Malachi 2:10.

[7] Isaiah 49:15; the "I" speaking is God.

[8] Amy-Jill Levine, *The Misunderstood Jew: The Church and the Scandal of the Jewish Jesus* (New York: HarperCollins, 2006), 44-45.

[9] Muriel Lester, *It Occurred to Me* (New York: Harper & Brothers, 1938), 278.

[10] Thomas Aquinas, Summa Theologiae 83:9, http://www.newadvent.org/summa/3083.htm#article9, accessed 4 April 2020.

The Holy Eucharist

I noticed the man during the rector's sermon that morning. Although I had served this church as associate rector for only a short time, his face was familiar. I saw him a couple of times a week in our church's parking lot or outside the shelter and community kitchen that backed up onto the parish hall. We would nod and say good morning. Although I kept small bills in my pocket to share with anyone who asked and always half-expected he might, he never did. Now, for the first time I knew of, he was attending our 11 o'clock celebration of the Holy Eucharist, and he was drunk.

I wouldn't have noticed the man during the sermon if he hadn't given my colleague a couple of out-loud "Amens" and a "Yes, Lord" or two. These responses set the visitor apart from the generally quiet congregation, but they didn't cause a stir. The service continued as usual.

What held my attention longer was the man's exclamation after I started distributing communion. "Jesus! I need my Jesus!" But as he stood up and took a step out of his pew, his knees buckled, and he thudded back down onto his seat. The people to his right, on the inside of the pew, stood by, clearly unsure what to do.

Then two of our ushers stepped up to the pew. One offered the man his arm, supporting his left side; when he stepped out into the aisle, the other usher took his right arm. Their bodies pressed tightly together, the trio moved to the chancel, up the steps, and then past the choir stalls to the altar rail. Seeing our visitor trembling, I stepped quickly, wafer in hand, to where they stood, but I hadn't reckoned with the man's determination to kneel. I waited as the ushers helped him down, dropped "the Body of Christ, the bread of heaven" into his outstretched hand, and then moved on as he received the cup.

That trio reminded me of a basic truth of the Christian life: we all need Jesus, and we find him—he finds us—as the community of disciples comes together in his name. If prayer is time consciously devoted to cultivating our relationship with God that has the potential to transform our souls, our lives, and the world, then the eucharist is both the foundation of all prayer and an incomparable experience of it. And Christians pray it together.

In his first letter to the Christians of Corinth, the Apostle Paul "handed on" what he had received from Jesus himself: "that the Lord Jesus on the night when he was betrayed took a loaf of bread, and when he had given thanks, he broke it and said, 'This is my body that is for you. Do this in remembrance of me.' In the same way he took the cup also, after supper, saying, 'This cup is the new covenant in my blood. Do this, as often as you drink it, in remembrance of me.' For as often as you eat this bread and drink the cup, you proclaim the Lord's death until he comes."[1] These couple of sentences, recorded around twenty years after Jesus's death and resurrection, have become what the church calls the "words of institution" of the eucharist. In this sacrament, Anglicans (and other branches of the church) affirm that Jesus Christ is truly present with us, uniting us not only to himself but also to all other members of his Body, and we trust that his presence in the bread and wine will spill over into our lives, shaping them more and more to resemble his. Or, as Augustine of Hippo said in a sermon on the eucharist, "Be what you see; receive what you are."[2]

The Book of Acts tells us that Christians began celebrating this feast, praying this prayer, soon after Jesus's resurrection.[3] It became the custom to gather on the first day of the week (what you and I call Sunday), the day when Jesus rose again, to remember his life, death, and resurrection. Early texts like the *Didache*, a first-century manual for the Christian life, and Justin Martyr's *First Apology* (meaning, a defense of the Christian faith) give outlines of the service that resemble what we celebrate today: reading scripture; praying for the congregation, its friends, and the world; collecting gifts of money (and perhaps other goods) to help members and strangers in need; thanking God for the gifts of bread and wine; blessing, breaking, and sharing those gifts among the baptized persons assembled, and sending away portions to those too ill or otherwise unable to attend.[4] The roots of the rite go back to the Jewish table blessing, which Jesus would have prayed over the bread and wine he shared with his closest friends, including the one who betrayed him, on the night before his execution. What was new in the Last Supper was that Jesus told his disciples that the bread and wine they shared *was his own body and blood* and that the meal they shared bound them, in some mysterious yet real way, to him and to each other beyond earthly life and death.

This binding together is what leads me to say that the whole eucharistic service, from the opening acclamation to the dismissal—and not just the part of the liturgy titled "the Eucharistic Prayer"—is a prayer.[5] The whole service, from beginning to end, is marked by the intention to bring the gathered community into Christ's presence, acknowledging how much we need him and thanking God for the fact that Jesus freely gives himself to his disciples who partake. Those who gather for the eucharist are Jesus's guests, whom he invited, longs to meet, and welcomes with his whole being. As former Archbishop of Canterbury Rowan Williams has written, "In Holy Communion, Jesus Christ tells us that he wants our company."[6] Jesus our Host resembles God walking in the Garden of Eden, calling out to the first humans, "Where are you?," anticipating the pleasure of passing time in conversation with them.

From the earliest days of the church, Christians have encountered Jesus Christ, our risen Lord, in this meal, like the disciples in Emmaus who recognized their traveling companion only after he took bread, blessed, broke, and gave it to them.[7] At the same time, in this rite, we remember his death, and we also express our trust that he will return; only God knows when. In a sense, when we gather for the eucharist, time collapses as we practice what the church, borrowing from Greek, calls *anamnesis*, or remembering. Anamnesis signifies a particular kind of remembering: recalling the past, not as an abstract recollection or a moment forever lost but as a living reality into which our collective prayer draws us and which equips us for life in a hoped-for future. As we relive the story of Jesus's final meal with his disciples, we proclaim that somehow, he is present with us, and we express our hope that we will enter fully into his presence after our own deaths.

On the night of his betrayal, Jesus told his disciples, "I will never again drink of this fruit of the vine until that day when I drink it new with you in my Father's kingdom."[8] He was invoking visions of the heavenly banquet painted by prophets like Isaiah, who promised,

> On this mountain the Lord of hosts will make for all peoples
> a feast of rich food, a feast of well-aged wines,
> of rich food filled with marrow,
> of well-aged wines strained clear.
> And he will destroy on this mountain
> the shroud that is cast over all peoples,
> the sheet that is spread over all nations;
> he will swallow up death forever.[9]

If we take Jesus at his word, the eucharist is sustenance for our earthly journey, to nourish us for life as his disciples until we feast with him and each other in the next life. Mother's milk is the closest analogy to this food, but as Julian of Norwich wrote in the fourteenth century, even that comparison falls short: "The mother can give her child to suck of her milk, but our precious Mother Jesus can feed us with himself, and does, most courteously and most tenderly, with the blessed sacrament, which is the precious food of true life."[10] The eucharist is closer to a divine transfusion of Jesus's presence, which has the capacity to form us into friends who can enjoy lingering at the table with him and each other rather than rushing off to betray him. And it is a foretaste of the heavenly feast he will share with his whole Body when the time comes. As Orthodox theologian Alexander Schmemann wrote of the eucharist, "If assembling as the church is, in the most profound sense of the term, the *beginning* of the eucharistic celebration…then its end and completion is the church's entrance into heaven, her fulfillment at the table of Christ, in his kingdom."[11] No living person has yet experienced that fulfillment, but our celebrations of the eucharist embody our longing for it while giving us little tastes of what we trust is to come.

Although communion is one of the two sacraments recognized by the entire church (the other being baptism), different communities celebrate it more or less often. Many Catholic churches, and some Episcopal ones, offer a daily eucharist, while many Protestant churches celebrate once a month or once a quarter. Until the late 1960s and 1970s (and for some parishes, into the 1980s), Episcopal churches generally fell into the latter category. But the liturgical renewal movement of the 1960s changed our practice. Scholars, laypersons, and clergy sought to make the church's liturgies, and our celebrations of them, more like the rites of the first Christian communities. The bishop or priest who presided at the eucharist had for centuries stood with their back to the congregation to signify leading them as they approached God together. With this liturgical renewal, the presiders now typically face the congregation from behind the holy table like a dinner host, recalling meals shared by the first house churches. A wider range of laypersons read lessons, help distribute communion, and perform other roles not specifically reserved for clergy. And the Episcopal Church has, since 1979, explicitly stated what early Christians took for granted: that the Holy Eucharist, not Morning Prayer or another service of the Word only, is to be "the principal act of Christian Worship on the Lord's Day and other major Feasts."[12] Today Anglicans generally assume that, unless some compelling reason is present, the faithful will gather on Sundays to share the bread and cup. For me, keeping the eucharist at the center of my prayer life reminds me that my deepest desire is to grow ever closer to Jesus. So close that his Body is incorporated into mine; so close that, I pray, my actions may grow to resemble his more and more over time.

The eucharist is by definition a prayer *of the church,* an enactment of our (not-yet-perfected) unity, meant to draw Christians closer to the Triune God and each other. That's why the default assumption in Christian liturgical theology is that a priest does not celebrate the eucharist alone.[13] The rite is written to be communal: "We confess"; "We lift [our hearts] up to the Lord; "We remember his death, we proclaim his resurrection, we await his coming in glory." And we symbolize the reconciliation Jesus effected between God and humanity by sharing a sign of peace—a kiss in the early church, more typically a handshake or a reverent bow today.

Because you and I are mortal, sinful creatures, the church embodies this reconciliation imperfectly at best. That's always been true. Paul's discussion of the Lord's Supper, in which he tells the church in Corinth, "I received from the Lord what I also handed onto you," comes not in the midst of a rapturous ode to spiritual unity, but rather in the middle of Paul's rebuke of the Corinthian church.

Having moved away to continue spreading the gospel, Paul had heard from sources back in Corinth that rich members of the congregation were flaunting their wealth in a most egregious way. In that time and place, a shared meal—a full supper—accompanied the distribution of communion bread and wine. Wealthy Christians in Corinth were bringing luxurious food to the gathering but only enough for themselves. Their poorer neighbors went hungry. Incensed by this news, Paul reprimanded his friends: "When you come together, it is not really to eat the Lord's supper. For when the time comes to eat, each of you goes ahead with your own supper, and one goes hungry and another becomes drunk. What! Do you not have homes to eat and drink in? Or do you show contempt for the church of God and humiliate those who have nothing?"[14]

The abuses Paul condemned didn't end with the church in Corinth. Even as the church has sought unity with Jesus through the eucharist, it has, over centuries, tolerated and even fomented sinful acts from the unkind to the horrifically violent. Most obviously and frequently, Christians have directed our violence against Jews: worshiping the Jewish Jesus and consuming his flesh while justifying the murders of Jewish people by the claim that the church had superseded Israel in God's favor.[15]

And in some cases, Christians have sacrificed beloved children of God to the eucharist. In the 1840s, when the bishop of North Carolina celebrated the fact that enslaved Black and free white persons took communion together, an abolitionist shared with the bishop a story from a self-liberated man. While attending a eucharist like those the bishop praised, the man, still enslaved at the time, had refused to partake, because his own brother had been sold to buy the new silver communion vessels.[16] By his refusal, that man exercised his Christian freedom even while he remained legally enslaved. He deployed an apostolic freedom like that with which Paul had rebuked the rich Corinthians, to let everyone around him know that sacrificing a human being in that manner constituted a blasphemous offense against the One who voluntarily became the first, last, and only human sacrifice acceptable to God.

A lot has changed since the mid-nineteenth century. Today, our congregations don't include slaveholders and enslaved persons like their antebellum forebears did. But many of the buildings in which white Americans worship, north and south, were built with profits from slavery. Some were built by enslaved persons themselves, without compensation or recognition. For some historically white congregations, reflecting on these realities has been a spur to self-examination and acts of restitution. For most, however, that process has yet to begin. One of my frequent prayers is that, as white Christians read and watch the news and also pray the eucharist together, the sacrament will impel us to examine our history and our consciences, to lament the injustices in which the church has been complicit, and to do everything we can to address those wrongs.

Beyond the ways in which such social sins have warped Christians' celebrations of the eucharist, every congregation is still marked by divisions from the petty to the weighty. The handshakes, kisses, and bows of the peace mask a wide variety of sins: the contests over music and service bulletins that divert church staffs and members from the meaningful ministries we share; the ways institutionalized racism benefits some Christians (like me) while slowly draining or violently snatching life from others; the presence of child abuse and domestic violence under our noses, although we protest they couldn't possibly be happening in our church. The fact that Christians aren't perfect and that we don't need to be perfect before approaching God may be why Pope Francis has so often referred to the church as "a field hospital,"[17] a place where wounds can be exposed and treated, so that healing may begin.

Healing is one of the benefits the eucharist offers. As the Catechism of the Episcopal Church teaches, "The benefits we receive [in the Lord's Supper] are the forgiveness of our sins, the strengthening of our union with Christ and one another, and the foretaste of the heavenly banquet which is our nourishment in eternal life."[18] We need this sacrament because we can't fulfill God's promises for ourselves. Left to our own devices, we will abuse our power and betray God, our neighbors, and ourselves. Jesus, betrayed by his friends and condemned to an agonizing death, knew that, and you and I know it too. That's why Christians return again and again, together, to the eucharist: to hear God's Word, to repent and confess our sins, to pray for our own needs and those of others, and finally, to bless, break, and share Jesus Christ's Body and Blood, remembering that none of us will be saved alone. And that's why we need an active life of prayer to uphold us between celebrations of the eucharist: to build on that foundation and, by grace, to shape our lives into gifts that are themselves blessed, broken, and shared out of love for our neighbor, and to the glory of God.

Questions to consider and things to try

✠ The next time you attend a eucharist, think of it intentionally as a time of prayer. What does it mean to you to pray in unison with a group of people? Are there people whose presence you appreciate more (such as a friend or a person with a pleasant voice) and some you appreciate less (such as your spouse with whom you exchanged sharp words on the way to church or a committee co-chair with whom you have been wrangling)? Notice these feelings without judging them; offer them to God, who drew you all together to this place of prayer.

✠ Is there a piece of the eucharistic prayer or a moment in the rite (such as the *sursum corda* or the fraction) that particularly catches your attention? Remember it, and contemplate it in prayer sometime during the week to come (perhaps finding it in the Book of Common Prayer, rereading and sitting with the words that struck you, or the words associated with the moment you especially noticed). Consider what that moment means to you and what gift it has to offer you.

✠ Learn something about the history of your church. Whom does it recognize as founders and benefactors? Where did the land, and funds needed to establish it, come from? What resources sustain it now? Who has, and has not, been welcome there, and to whom are the church buildings and services accessible? What impact does learning this history have on you and your fellow congregants, and on your sense of unity with fellow Christians?

✠ Consider supplementing your regular Bible with *The Jewish Annotated New Testament*.[19] An important corrective to the unwitting anti-Semitism that still permeates the church, our preaching, and our celebration of the sacraments, it contains notes and essays by Jewish scholars of the New Testament.

✠ If the eucharist is heavenly food for our earthly journey, what is it feeding you for today, or this week or month? What nourishment or strength do you need, and for what purpose?

Endnotes

[1] 1 Corinthians 11:23-26.

[2] Augustine of Hippo, Sermon 272, "On the Nature of the Sacrament of the Eucharist," https://earlychurchtexts.com/public/augustine_sermon_272_eucharist.htm, accessed 12 December 2020.

[3] See Acts 2:42-43 and 20:7.

[4] Aaron Milavec, *The Didache: Text, Translation, Analysis, and Commentary* (Collegeville, MN: Liturgical Press, 2003), 9:1-10:7. Justin Martyr's outline of eucharistic celebration is in Chapters 65-67 of his First Apology, https://www.newadvent.org/fathers/0126.htm, accessed 3 October 2020.

[5] The opening acclamation is the celebrant's greeting to the people and their response, e.g. "Blessed be God: Father, Son, and Holy Spirit; And blessed be his kingdom, now and for ever; Amen" (The Book of Common Prayer, 355), and the dismissal is the final words of the service, e.g. "Let us go forth in the name of Christ; Thanks be to God" (The Book of Common Prayer, 366).

[6] Rowan Williams, *Being Christian: Baptism, Bible, Eucharist, Prayer* (Grand Rapids, MI: William B. Eerdmans Publishing Co., 2014), 41.

[7] Luke 24:13-35.

[8] Matthew 26:29; also Mark 14:25 and Luke 22:18.

[9] Isaiah 25:6-8. "This mountain" is presumably Mount Zion, traditionally understood as the dwelling place of the God of Israel and the center of the world.

[10] Julian of Norwich, Edmund Colledge, OSA, and James Walsh, SJ, *Julian of Norwich: Showings* (Mahwah, NJ: Paulist Press, 1978), 298.

[11] Alexander Schmemann, *The Eucharist: Sacrament of the Kingdom*, trans. Paul Kachur (Crestwood, NY: St. Vladimir's Seminary Press, 2000), 27.

[12] The Book of Common Prayer, 13. I discuss Morning Prayer in the chapter on the Daily Office.

[13] Roman Catholic priests can celebrate alone if necessary, but the norm is to have at least one other person present.

[14] 1 Corinthians 11:20-22a.

[15] Lauren F. Winner discusses anti-Jewish violence rooted in the eucharist in *The Dangers of Christian Practice: On Wayward Gifts, Characteristic Damage, and Sin* (New Haven: Yale University Press, 2018).

[16] William Jay, *A Letter to the Right Rev. L. Silliman Ives, Bishop of the Protestant Episcopal Church in the State of North Carolina, Occasioned by his late Address to the Convention of his Diocese. By a Protestant Episcopalian* (Washington, D.C.: Buell and Blanchard, 1846), 7,9. Cited in The Rev. Dr. Brooks Graebner, "One great fellowship of love? Theological convictions & ecclesial realities in the racial history of the Diocese of North Carolina—Address delivered to the Annual Convention of the Diocese, 16 November 2017," 3.

[17] For example, in Antonio Spadaro, S.J., "A Big Heart Open to God: An Interview with Pope Francis," *America: The Jesuit Review*, September 30, 2013, https://www.americamagazine.org/faith/2013/09/30/big-heart-open-god-interview-pope-francis, accessed 13 December 2020.

[18] The Book of Common Prayer, 859-860.

[19] Amy-Jill Levine and Marc Zvi Brettler, eds., *The Jewish Annotated New Testament, 2nd Ed.* (New York: Oxford University Press, 2017).

The Daily Office

The Daily Office is an old-fashioned term that has nothing to do with commuting to a building to work and everything to do with remembering that we pass our days in the company of God and the saints. What Anglicans call "the Daily Office," Roman Catholics know as "the Divine Office" or "the Liturgy of the Hours." They are simply set prayers said at certain times of the day. The word "office," used in this way, refers to a duty one holds, something one does, especially on behalf of others, because of who one is—in this case, a disciple of Jesus Christ. In the Anglican tradition, the offices, or prayer services, are four: Morning Prayer, Noonday Prayer, Evening Prayer, and Compline. This daily cycle moves through a prescribed set of prayers and scripture readings (much shorter in Noonday Prayer and Compline than the other two services), while leaving space for personal intercessions and thanksgivings. If you prayed Morning and Evening Prayer daily for three years, you would read most of the Bible in that time. You would experience all the varied moods of the church year: from the expectant self-examination of Advent, the joy of Christmas and Epiphany, the penitence of Lent and resurrection promise of Easter, and the empowerment and call to discipleship of Pentecost and the long season after that feast. Over the course of weeks and months, the Daily Office would shape your sense of self and your knowledge of God and perhaps even transform your concept of time and the boundaries of community.

My experience of praying the Daily Office is inseparable from the two main places I have prayed it.

The first place is the tiny urban church I served as vicar for a few years, shortly after my ordination. That parish's Daily Office started as one parishioner praying Morning Prayer every Monday through Friday, alone except for the days when I or someone else stopped by. That "someone else" was often a member of the small community of homeless men who lived on the church grounds, a couple of miles from the nearest community kitchen. So, after a while, we added a post-prayer breakfast to our morning ritual, gathering around a table in the parish hall and taking plates out to parking-lot residents to ease their transition from a night passed on asphalt to the new day. The institution of breakfast brought in not just more of our homeless neighbors but also more members of our congregation and Presbyterians from the church across the street.

When we added Evening Prayer to the daily schedule, workers on their way home from nearby Duke Hospital started stopping in. Only one was an Episcopalian who attended another parish on Sundays; most were simply seeking a quiet place (usually a back pew) to rest, leave behind the worries of the day, and gather strength or ask for help in whatever way made sense to them. I rarely officiated these lay-led services but would slide into a pew as the service started, smiling at my parishioners' familiar voices repeating the prayers that, over time, so many of us learned by heart. In the morning, the *Magnificat*—"He has filled the hungry with good things, and the rich he has sent away empty"—and in the evening, the *Nunc Dimittis*— "For these eyes of mine have seen the Savior, whom you have prepared for all the world to see"—spoke truth about the community we were trying to weave at the church. And the prayers encouraged us to keep going, to keep listening for guidance about how best to love God, our neighbors, and ourselves.

The second place is my back porch, one mile from that church. Most days, during my tenure as vicar, I would get up early to write. On all but the coldest mornings in North Carolina's sub-tropical climate, I would greet the sunrise alone with a cup of coffee, facing the backyard. There, I had arranged feeders of all kinds and planted seed- and fruit-bearing plants in a campaign to attract the widest variety of birds possible. Chickadees trilled their eponymous calls, wrens sang duets, wily blue jays imitated hawks in attempts to scare away their smaller competitors, and squirrels performed Cirque du Soleil-worthy acrobatics in their attempts to shake loose seed from various feeding stations. These creatures had no idea they served as my choir and congregation as I prayed, "For the Lord is a great God, and a great King above all gods. In his hand are the caverns of the earth, and the heights of the hills are his also," or "Be joyful in the Lord, all you lands; serve the Lord with gladness and come before his presence with a song." They knew nothing of church squabbles over matters too insignificant even to recall now or of anguished conversations about how those of us who had houses might best love our neighbors who slept outside. They glorified God simply by living, by being who our Creator made them to be. My prayer on that back porch was, and still is, one way to follow their example.

The tradition of praying at set times of the day comes from the Bible and the communities that produced it, inspired by, and in conversation with, God. Psalm 55 tells of calling on God "in the evening, in the morning, and at noonday," which became the pattern for thrice-daily traditional Jewish prayers. From Psalm 119, we hear (the probably metaphorical) "Seven times a day do I praise you,"[1] which inspired early Christian monastic practices. Writing his new religious order's rule of life in the early sixth century, Saint Benedict cited that verse as the basis for monks' obligation to pray seven services at set times through the day and night.[2]

But the prayer offices aren't just for monks and nuns. As early as the second century, Christian communities adopted the habit of marking different moments of the day with communal and private prayers for the church and the world. Clergy and laypersons whose work schedules allowed were expected to participate.[3] While the English Reformers dissolved their country's monasteries, the Book of Common Prayer offered services of Morning and Evening Prayer (also known as Matins and Vespers) to be celebrated in churches and in homes. In the Reformers' ideal vision of the household, its head, usually the father, would act as family abbot. In these twice-daily services, he would lead his wife and children—and the servants it was assumed he would employ if he were prosperous enough to be literate. Regardless of whether a family observed these times of household prayer, English Christians became familiar with the Daily Office. At a time when communion might be received only a few times a year, Morning Prayer was, for much of Anglican history, the principal service prayed corporately at church on Sunday. In many churches, both the morning and evening offices were sung, and a rich choral tradition grew up around the offices.

In the United States and around the Anglican world, Morning Prayer remained the principal service of the Lord's Day well into the twentieth century. Episcopalians who grew up with the 1928 prayer book became deeply familiar with the service's rhythms—opening prayers, reading, canticle, reading, canticle—even though they might not pray it the other six days a week. But the 1979 Book of Common Prayer reshaped the church's practice, re-emphasizing baptism as the center of our theology and re-establishing the eucharist as the normative Sunday service. Only a minority of churches continued to hold services of Morning or Evening Prayer on weekdays. As a result, the Daily Office became, to many Episcopalians, an unfamiliar part of their faith heritage.

That started to change during the novel coronavirus pandemic of 2020. As limits on public gatherings made it impossible for congregations to gather to celebrate the eucharist, many turned to services of Morning Prayer on Sundays, livestreamed or held over videoconference. Weekday lunchtimes and late evenings found clergy and lay ministers officiating Noonday Prayer and Compline over Facebook Live, taking prayer requests from comment boxes as participants sent "like," "love," and prayer-hands emojis into the ether to signal their participation. Earlier generations of Christians would be mystified by these technological changes, but they would understand the need to feel connected to God and other people through prayer, and they would recognize many pieces of the prayer offices we still use.

Like the eucharist, the Daily Office weaves together every type of prayer: adoration, praise, thanksgiving, penitence, oblation, intercession, and petition. It does this mainly by snipping together words from scripture and the tradition, whose sources you might not recognize at first but that become more and more familiar as you move through the Daily Office's prescribed readings. So even on days when I may be feeling uncharitable toward the church or hopeless about the future of my country, I know Morning Prayer will prompt me to offer, "Clothe your ministers with righteousness; Let your people sing with joy…Lord, keep this nation under your care; And guide us in the way of justice and truth" (The Book of Common Prayer, 97-98).[4] The Lord's Prayer, included in every office, reminds me to return to Jesus, that he will give me words to pray when I have none. The confession—optional at the beginning of both Morning and Evening Prayer, but especially appropriate in Advent and Lent— nudges me to face the truth that, even before breakfast, I and my fellow Christians "have not loved [God] with our whole heart; we have not loved our neighbors as ourselves" (The Book of Common Prayer, 79). Left to my own devices, I might leave out one form of prayer or another, praying only for myself and not for my neighbors or wallowing in self-recrimination without remembering to pray for my own needs or to praise God for loving me as I am.

Over time, as with the eucharist, pieces of the Daily Office have become part of me. I often find myself repeating pieces of the canticles (pieces of scripture arranged to be sung or recited as poetry). When I need courage or comfort, the First Song of Isaiah comes to my lips: "Surely, it is God who saves me; I will trust in him and not be afraid. For the Lord is my stronghold and my sure defense, and he will be my Savior" (The Book of Common Prayer, 86).

When the pain of the headlines is too much, and I need to close my eyes for a moment, A Song of Praise reminds me to fix my gaze on God who resurrected Jesus and is still making all things new, hard as that may be to believe sometimes: "Glory to you, Lord God of our fathers[5]; you are worthy of praise, glory to you. Glory to you for the radiance of your holy Name; we will praise you and highly exalt you forever" (The Book of Common Prayer, 90).

Even on nights when I don't pray the full service of Compline, the last words on my lips before sleep are one of its closing prayers, composed by Saint Augustine of Hippo: "Keep watch, dear Lord, with those who work, or watch, or weep this night, and give your angels charge over those who sleep. Tend the sick, Lord Christ; give rest to the weary, bless the dying, soothe the suffering, pity the afflicted, shield the joyous; and all for your love's sake" (The Book of Common Prayer, 134).

As we repeat these prayers, we are meant to take them into ourselves, to ingest them, using a dietary metaphor, and let them nourish us for a life of discipleship. How will we know when they have fed us in this way? When the church's prayers change the way we live. When I pray, "Lord, keep us from all sin today" (The Book of Common Prayer, 98), I don't just mean "that sinner" over there: the politician I can't see ushered out fast enough or the family member with whom I can hardly bear to share a holiday meal. I have to mean us: me and every other sinner whom God loves and who stands in need of God's forgiveness. And I have to ask myself, what am I doing in my waking hours to give rest to the weary, bless the dying, and soothe the suffering? If I take the *Magnificat* to heart, it will remind me every time I pray it, and as I go about my day, that God the Father of Jesus Christ is the one who scatters the proud (who could be me) in their conceit, casts down the mighty from their thrones and lifts up the lowly, fills the hungry with good things and sends the rich (compared to most people on the planet, that's definitely me) away empty (The Book of Common Prayer, 92). If Mary's song echoes through my mind and heart from the outset of my day, I stand a better chance of acting in ways that reveal me, and in turn shape me, to be a follower of her Son.

There's a reason my last two statements start with "If." Beloved by God that I am, I'm also a sinner, as prone to self-deception as anyone else. It would be entirely possible for me to pray the Daily Office scrupulously, repeating the words until I could recite them by rote, without taking time to examine my own soul and my daily actions in light of the prayers' vision of God. In his classic book, *Beginning to Pray,* the Orthodox monk and bishop Anthony Bloom warns of this danger. He says the Orthodox Morning and Evening Prayers should take about half an hour, twice a day, to read, about the same as the equivalent Anglican prayers, if one occasionally stops to reflect. "A person," Bloom notes, "will try to learn them by heart so that at other moments he or she can draw from them. But it is not enough just to learn prayers by heart. A prayer makes sense only if it is lived. Unless they are 'lived,' unless life and prayer become completely interwoven, prayers become a sort of polite madrigal which you offer to God at moments when you are giving time to Him."[6] The Daily Office follows set patterns, but it's not just a performance (although offered corporately, it is, in part, a performance that can be executed more or less beautifully). It's a framework we can use to devote time to God, letting the words of scripture and tradition shape us—slowly, eventually—into people who know God more fully as Parent, Friend, and Lover of us all.

So how might one start to pray the Daily Office?

Many people feel overwhelmed when they first open the Book of Common Prayer to the service of Morning Prayer. The service can start with confession, or without; the opening verses and the antiphons (choruses, essentially) to the psalms vary with the seasons; and you need to learn how to find the day's scripture readings in the lectionary (the list of prescribed readings for each day) at the back of the prayer book. All the instructions you need are contained within the prayer book, in the rubrics (the directions in italic type that appear throughout all the prayer book's services), in the "Additional Directions" starting on page 141, and in the lectionary instructions beginning on page 934. All of these well-intended directions, however, can feel ironically confusing.

That's why it's often easiest to apprentice with another person. There might be a church near you that prays one or more of the offices daily, where you can follow along with someone who's been attending for a while. If the service is online, the person officiating will likely lead the congregation through it page by page. You might ask your priest, or another experienced office pray-er, to guide you through the service, and you could mark up your prayer book with notes, suggestions, and hints.

Or you could use one of several shortcuts or aids to prayer:

✚ Connect to Forward Movement's "Daily Prayer Anytime" site, which will lead you through any or all of the four daily services, with scripture readings already plugged in: prayer.forwardmovement.org/daily_prayer_anytime.php

✚ Use another reliable website based on the Book of Common Prayer, such as The Mission of St. Clare: missionstclare.com/english/

✚ Start with "Daily Devotions for Individuals and Families," the prayer book's abbreviated versions of the offices.

If setting aside a specific time for prayer each day is a new practice for you, I suggest starting, not with Morning or Evening Prayer, but with one of the simpler offices, Noonday Prayer (officially called "An Order of Service for Noonday," The Book of Common Prayer, 103) or Compline (The Book of Common Prayer, 127). This would give you a chance to get into the habit of praying in a certain set form, at a general time of day (noon to three p.m., traditionally, for the midday office, and sometime after dinner for Compline), before diving into the longer morning and evening offices.

Whatever office you pray, pray it *out loud* as you are able. Don't just read the words in your head. Speaking the words out loud reminds us that we're not reading the Book of Common Prayer for information. We're engaging in a conversation that our elders in faith have been having for a very long time and in which our Christian siblings engage today. Speaking the prayers aloud may feel strange at first, but with time, the practice will become familiar.

Something else will feel strange, if you pray these services alone, as many of us do: saying the word "us," as in Compline's, "The Lord Almighty grant us a peaceful night and a perfect end." If it does feel uncomfortable or out of place, remember why the prayer book is titled the Book of *Common* Prayer: in praying its services, for your own good and that of others, you are never truly alone. Other Anglicans around the world are praying, too, each in their time zones and languages but in mutually recognizable forms. We're also praying for the people in our lives and in our churches who, for whatever reason, cannot or will not pray. As a member of the communion of saints, "knit together," as the prayer for All Saints' Day says, "in one communion and fellowship in the mystical body of your Son Christ our Lord," you pray with and for other Christians, in this life and the next, as we seek a closer union with God, our common Source.

Questions to consider and things to try

✤ Pick one of the four offices and pray it daily for anywhere from a week to a month. As often as you can in that time, jot down a few notes about the experience: What feels strange? What feels welcome or just right? What prayers of intercession, petition, or thanksgiving arise in you as you pray within this framework?

> *You might ask a friend to take up this practice with you, either praying together (physically or through the use of technology) or being accountable to each other for your daily practice.*

✤ Look through the "Prayers and Thanksgivings" starting on page 810 of the Book of Common Prayer. If any particularly resonate with you, add them to your daily prayer practice, or mark them to use on appropriate occasions. You might learn one or two by heart and recite them at certain times of the day, as I do with Saint Augustine's prayer from Compline.

✤ As you pray Morning and/or Evening Prayer for weeks or months, notice if anything about your relationship to scripture changes. Are you reading books of the Bible that were unfamiliar to you? Are you hearing familiar stories in new ways? You might seek out a Bible study group as a conversation partner. You might also invest in a study Bible and a one-volume Bible commentary to give you some historical and theological background. *The New Oxford Annotated Bible* and *The Harper Collins Study Bible* are reliable, as is *Harper Collins Bible Commentary*.

Endnotes

[1] The evening is listed as the first moment of prayer because Jewish days start at sundown of the previous day. The number seven in the Bible often indicates completeness, so that Psalm 119 could be referring to constant prayer rather than seven distinct periods of prayer.

[2] Timothy Fry, OSB, ed., *The Rule of St. Benedict in English* (Collegeville, MN: The Liturgical Press, 1982), 16:1-3.

[3] Marion J. Hatchett, *Commentary on the American Prayer Book* (New York: HarperOne, 1995), 89.

[4] If you don't have a printed Book of Common Prayer, a full-text version, with the same pagination as the print version, can be found at https://bcponline.org/.

[5] The original Greek of this prayer could also be translated by the gender-inclusive "ancestors."

[6] Anthony Bloom, *Beginning to Pray* (Mahwah, NJ: Paulist Press, 1970), 59.

Praying the Psalms

The troubled singer of Psalm 88 opens with an anguished address: "O Lord, my God, my Savior, by day and night I cry to you."[1] They describe their misery: "For I am full of trouble; my life is at the brink of the grave." They affirm that their anguish is no fleeting discomfort: "Ever since my youth, I have been wretched and at the point of death; I have borne your terrors with a troubled mind." And they end on an utterly bleak note: "My friend and my neighbor you have put away from me, and darkness is my only companion."[2]

You might be surprised to learn that such a hopeless cry of pain is one of my very favorite psalms. It has resonated with me since the first time I read it, some months after my mother's death. By that time, I already knew by heart the lament she had composed, herself, in the hour before she died.

"I can no longer cope with the loneliness. At this point, the future could not look any blacker. I do not want to become an emotional burden to anyone—I simply can't go on—I kept thinking I could work my way out of this horrible depression that grips me, but I can't do it…"

I doubt my mother was familiar with any psalm other than Psalm 23, which she memorized in Sunday school as a child. But as she prepared to end her own life, a middle-aged woman whose entire adult existence had been shaped by depression, she unknowingly echoed a prayer composed millennia before and deemed worthy to include in the canon of writings holy first to Jews, and then to Christians.

Its inclusion in the Bible is what makes me love Psalm 88 so. If the agony that can cause a person to snuff out their own life can find a place within the record of God's saving love, then surely, no human emotion needs to be held back from God. Whatever you and I may feel, we can pray.[3]

Christians pray the psalms because Jesus did. Called *Tehilim*, "songs of praise," in the original Hebrew and traditionally ascribed to King David (who may have written some of them), the psalter was composed by a variety of poets over more than half a millennium, and some of its songs have roots in even older, polytheistic poetry of Israel's neighbors.[4] By the fifth or fourth century BCE, the book looked more or less as we now know it. Jesus would have heard the psalms sung in synagogues and in the temple, and the gospels tell us that he used them both to illuminate who he was, "The stone that the builders rejected has become the chief cornerstone" (Psalm 118); and to cry out in agony from the cross, "My God, my God, why have you forsaken me?" (Psalm 22). Even Satan quoted Psalm 91 in an attempt to convince Jesus to throw himself off the pinnacle of the temple: "For he will command his angels concerning you…On their hands they will bear you up, so that you will not dash your foot against a stone." There would have been no point in the Tempter citing that promise if Jesus had not been familiar with the passage in question. (Jesus also knew the Torah and so was able to retort from Deuteronomy, "Do not put the Lord your God to the test.")

As the church developed, the scriptures of Israel were the new community's sacred writings too, and the psalms held a particularly important place in disciples' communal liturgies and personal prayers. From the opening line of Augustine's *Confessions*, "Great are you, O Lord, and exceedingly worthy of praise; your power is immense, and your wisdom beyond reckoning," the fourth-century Bishop of Hippo invokes the psalms at least seventy times, far more than any other book of scripture, using these ancient hymns to extol God as Creator of the universe and Lover of each human soul. Protestant reformer John Calvin recommended the psalms as a school for prayer: "In short, as calling upon God is one of the principal means of securing our safety, and as a better and more unerring rule for guiding us in this exercise cannot be found elsewhere than in the psalms, it follows, that in proportion to the proficiency which a [person] shall have attained in understanding them, will be [their] knowledge of the most important part of celestial doctrine."[5]

Our ancestors in faith knew that the psalms could teach you and me about the relationship among God, us, and our neighbors (the non-human ones as well as the humans); show us how to pray; and articulate our prayer when our own words fail. Most of the psalms can be classified as laments or thanksgivings, but they also serve other purposes: praise, penitence, instruction.[6]

When we're feeling utterly abandoned to our troubles, we can find a grief-stricken companion in Psalm 13:

> How long, O LORD?
> will you forget me for ever?
>> how long will you hide your face from me?

When we're overflowing with gratitude, especially after coming through hard times, we might turn to Psalm 30:

> O LORD my God, I cried out to you,
>> and you restored me to health.

You brought me up, O LORD, from the dead;
>   you restored my life as I was going down to the grave.

Others, like Psalm 117 (just two verses long), are useful when we want to praise God or when we need a reminder that God is worthy of praise:

>   Praise the LORD, all you nations;
>   laud him, all you peoples.

>   For his loving-kindness toward us is great,
>   and the faithfulness of the LORD endures forever.
>   Hallelujah!

When we need help expressing remorse, we can turn to the penitential psalms. Psalm 51 is so appropriate to this purpose that it serves as the introduction to the Book of Common Prayer's Rite of Reconciliation of a Penitent:

>   Have mercy on me, O God, according to your
>   loving-kindness;
>   in your great compassion blot out my offenses.

>   Wash me through and through from my wickedness,
>   and cleanse me from my sin.

>   For I know my transgressions,
>   and my sin is ever before me.

And when we need guidance for life, help to put today's headlines into a context as broad as millennia, psalms like 49 have wisdom to offer; wisdom that can comfort or warn us, depending on our behavior:

>   Why should I be afraid in evil days,
>   when the wickedness of those at my heels surrounds me,

>   The wickedness of those who put their trust in their goods,
>   and boast of their great riches?

We can never ransom ourselves,
　　or deliver to God the price of our life;

For the ransom of our life is so great,
　　that we should never have enough to pay it,

In order to live for ever and ever,
　　and never see the grave.

Occasionally, these wisdom psalms preview sayings of Jesus that are more familiar to Christians. Jesus seems to have repurposed the tenth verse of Psalm 37, "For evildoers shall be cut off, but those who wait upon the Lord shall possess the land" for his promise, "Blessed are the meek, for they shall inherit the earth" (Matthew 5:5). And sometimes, when I pray the psalms I find myself arguing with the original composer, who a few verses later in this psalm muses, "I have been young and now I am old, but never have I seen the righteous forsaken, or their children begging bread." (I have.)

What gives the psalms this emotional impact that resonates through millennia of human experience across vastly differing cultures? In large part, it's the vivid, sharply physical images they offer.

The singer in despair about the ways in which shameless people take advantage of the poor mourns in Psalm 10,

[The wicked] lie in wait, like a lion in a covert;
they lie in wait to seize upon the lowly;
　　they seize the lowly and drag them away in their net.

In Psalm 3, the psalmist, desperate for vindication, cries out,

Rise up, O Lord; set me free, O my God;
　　surely, you will strike all my enemies across the face;
　　you will break the teeth of the wicked.

Psalm 14 presents the image of teeth to symbolize the damage done by people who misuse their power:

> Have they no knowledge, all those evildoers
>> who eat up my people like bread
>> and do not call upon the LORD?

Those evildoers should beware, for in Psalm 68, "God shall crush the heads of his enemies, and the hairy scalp of those who go on still in their wickedness."

One who feels the Lord is far off, but who dares to hope for comfort might pray, "As the deer longs for the water-brooks, so longs my soul for you, O God" (Psalm 42:1) or, "You [God] have noted my lamentation; put my tears into your bottle; are they not recorded in your book?" (Psalm 56:8).

Occasionally, God's voice uses these vivid images to rebuke people who worship as their faith requires—sacrificing animals in the ancient world; regular church attendance, in ours—but who won't make the emotional sacrifices loving their neighbors requires. In Psalm 50, we hear:

> If I were hungry, I would not tell you,
>> for the whole world is mine and all that is in it.

> Do you think I eat the flesh of bulls,
>> or drink the blood of goats?

It's precisely the vividness of these images that tends to make Christians uncomfortable with some psalms. The laments can seem too raw to hold safely in our mouths, and those we call "imprecatory," that wish harm to enemies, can make us wonder nervously whether it's appropriate for disciples of Jesus, the Prince of Peace, to pray these words. That's why imprecatory verses are routinely left out of the lectionary's psalm selections, and the deepest laments, like Psalm 88, appear rarely.[7]

To me, these difficult psalms are some of the most valuable: signs that God's grace is soil rich enough to receive our saltiest tears and most poisonous desires and transform them into nourishing fruit to strengthen us for the challenging work of discipleship.

Explore these prayers with me, and see if you agree.

The psalm that, arguably, makes Christians the most nervous is Psalm 137. A rare psalm set in a specific time and place, remembering Israel's defeat by the Babylonian Empire in the sixth century BCE, its opening is familiar to many: "By the waters of Babylon we sat down and wept, when we remembered you, O Zion." Further verses elicit sympathy for the people driven away from their homeland into foreign captivity, dislocated and bewildered:

> For those who led us away captive asked us for a song,
> and our oppressors called for mirth:
>> "Sing us one of the songs of Zion."
>
> How shall we sing the LORD's song
> upon an alien soil?

But in the final two verses, when the psalmist lets loose their rawest feelings, they lose many of us:

> O Daughter of Babylon, doomed to destruction,
> happy the one who pays you back
> for what you have done to us!
>
> Happy shall be he who takes your little ones,
> and dashes them against the rock!

Dreaming of taking revenge by spilling the brains of your enemies' children. Could there be a less Christian sentiment?

I think that question is the wrong one to ask here. "Will you trust me with the story that moved you to sing this song of vengeance?" might be a more appropriate query. Instead of judging the one who prays so, Psalm 137 invites us to stand beside them: to hear their deep grief and rage as they lament husbands and sons lost in battle and babies miscarried on the forced march away from home, as they grapple with the shock of being uprooted from family, community, and a landscape they will never see again.

It has always been easier for people who have experienced oppression not only to stand beside the singer of Psalm 137 but even to put themselves in the original pray-er's shoes—or chains. Frederick Douglass, the African American abolitionist who liberated himself from slavery, referred to this psalm in his 1852 speech, "What to the Slave is the Fourth of July?" Douglass reminded his white listeners that although they might celebrate the anniversary of their country's independence, he could not. Instead, he declared, "I can to-day take up the plaintive lament of a peeled and woe-smitten people!" continuing, "By the rivers of Babylon, there we sat down. Yea! we wept when we remembered Zion. We hanged our harps upon the willows in the midst thereof. For there, they that carried us away captive, required of us a song…Fellow-citizens, above your national, tumultuous joy, I hear the mournful wail of millions! whose chains, heavy and grievous yesterday, are, to-day, rendered more intolerable by the jubilee shouts that reach them."[8] Identifying with God's captive people across time and space strengthened Douglass for his struggle on two fronts: against slaveholders and the government that protected their interests, and to open the eyes of white Americans, including those who considered themselves above reproach because they owned no slaves.

Almost two centuries later, Nobel-prize-winning novelist Toni Morrison, an intellectual heir to Douglass's tradition of truth-telling, told a British newspaper, "People keep saying, 'We need to have a conversation about race.' This is the conversation. I want to see a cop shoot a white unarmed teenager in the back. And I want to see a white man convicted for raping a black woman. Then when you ask me, 'Is it over?', I will say yes."[9] Speaking in the spring of 2015, Morrison likely had in mind unarmed adolescents and young men like Trayvon Martin, killed by a self-deputized neighbor who saw Trayvon, walking to his father's suburban home, as a threat; Eric Garner, who died in the process of being arrested for selling loose cigarettes, having repeated "I can't breathe" at least 11 times in a police officer's chokehold; and Michael Brown, shot to death by Ferguson, Missouri, police after being stopped for walking in the street. Morrison may also have been thinking of the fact that no one was ever convicted of any of these killings.

Morrison's words have shocked a lot of people, most of them white. But those who are shocked might search their souls for answers to the questions implied in her statement about a "conversation about race." What is the price, the value, of a Black person's life, more than a century after Emancipation? Where will justice come from when the perpetrator of violence can't, or won't, admit they did anything wrong? How can one group of Christians celebrate, or take for granted, their freedom while remaining oblivious to the pain of their neighbors still in chains, either literal or figurative?

These are the questions the imprecatory psalms howl to anyone who will listen.

These harsh verses remind us, too, when we are filled with rage toward someone who has harmed us (or who we think has harmed us; sometimes we're mistaken), that there is no part of us too ugly, no face too purple with anger or too stained with tears, to bare to God. Whatever revenge fantasies these prayers might indulge, in the end, they have sober, loving reminders for us: that Christians must listen to the stories of those who are wronged, and that even as we seek restitution for wrongs, ultimate justice is God's to mete out. That it is better to pray these things than to do them and stain our own hands and souls with violence; that howling to God about those who have debased themselves by oppressing others may keep us from debasing ourselves by sinning in response. And that maybe, by praying it out, our anger will be purged, refined, and redirected toward living well, showing as much charity toward our neighbors and as much self-respect as God-given grace and strength will allow.

The psalms are prayers we can turn to again and again, not only in our everyday devotions but in those moments when our own emotional and linguistic reserves are depleted. They offer an affirmation, as I found in Psalm 88, that God sees one's suffering or the suffering of one's beloved. Far from denying the depths of human sin and suffering, they testify vividly to it, and at the same time, they witness to the hope God offers. Commenting on Psalm 130's line, "I wait for the Lord; my soul waits for him; in his word is my hope" in light of her experience with bipolar disorder, Episcopal priest and theologian Kathryn Greene-McCreight writes, "Waiting on the Lord when one is mentally ill takes extreme effort….It was only through reading the Bible and the prayers of others, in particular the psalms, that I came to be able to wait, to hope in God's plenteous redemption. Or at least to acknowledge that some had that hope and that I wanted to be in the community that had that hope, even if I could not feel it."[10]

The book of *Tehilim*, of praises, is aptly named. The fact that we are invited to offer our every emotion to God is cause for praise. So is the psalms' encouragement to tell truth, to consider truth from the point of view of someone who carries a burden we don't, and to remember we do not shoulder our own burdens alone. If we can do all that within a community that will, as Paul wrote in Romans 12:15, rejoice with those who rejoice and weep with those who weep, then our praises will be multiplied.

Questions to consider and things to try

✠ Every day for a week, pray the lectionary psalm(s) of the day or the psalm from the previous or upcoming Sunday.

✠ Notice the images, the emotions, that particularly catch your attention.

> *Notice how relationships are described. Do these relationships teach you anything about how to live your own life? Do some of them seem more appropriate to biblical times than to the twenty-first century?*

> *Have you been in the position the psalmist describes? If not, can you imagine who might be?*

> *As you pray the psalm, do you hear a word God might be offering you in this moment?*

> *Consider praying this way for another week and compare the experiences.*

✠ Pray the psalms in the thirty-day cycle laid out in the Book of Common Prayer, following the sequence from "First Day: Morning Prayer" beginning on page 585, through "Thirtieth Day: Evening Prayer" beginning on page 804.

> *What does this experience of praying the entire psalter teach you?*

> *Are there psalms you want to linger over or others you would prefer to avoid? You might want to revisit both of those.*

> *Are there aspects of the psalms' theology that don't seem to match your Christian faith? You might discuss these with a friend or in a small group to see how your perspectives are similar or different.*

✠ When the Sunday or daily lectionary leaves out verses from certain psalms, look up the missing verses in the Book of Common Prayer or the Bible. What might we lose when the psalms are abridged in this way? Do we gain anything?

✠ As you read or watch the news or encounter a political situation that seems unendurable, write an imprecatory psalm about it. See what insights you gain through the process about yourself, God, and the people you are praying against and for. Does this reflection move you to further prayer, conversation with a friend or neighbor, or other non-violent action?

Endnotes

[1] Unless otherwise noted, psalm texts come from the Book of Common Prayer 1979.

[2] Scholar Robert Alter notes that in the original terse Hebrew, the final line sounds even more fragmented as if the singer is no longer capable of forming a coherent utterance: "My friends—utter darkness" (just two words in the original). "The sense," Alter observes, "is that either that the speaker's friends, because they have rejected him and withdrawn their presence from him, are nothing but darkness to him, or that now" (as the Book of Common Prayer states) "the only 'friend' he has is darkness." Robert Alter, *The Book of Psalms: A Translation with Commentary* (New York: W.W. Norton and Co., 2007), 310.

[3] If you need support to hold onto life or are grieving a loss by suicide, please reach out to your clergyperson, doctor, or other trusted contact, or to the American Foundation for Suicide Prevention at https://afsp.org/. If you are not struggling with this issue, please remember that depression and grief can make it extremely difficult for people to reach out for help, and be in touch with friends and neighbors who may be in pain. AFSP offers resources for people who want to be supportive.

[4] Alter, *The Book of Psalms*, xiii-xv.

[5] John Calvin, *Commentary on the Book of Psalms*, p. xxxvii. https://calvin.edu/centers-institutes/meeter-center/files/john-calvins-works-in-english/Commentary%20008%20-%20Psalms%20Vol.%201.pdf, accessed 9 August 2020.

[6] Different scholars sort the psalms into different categories. All of these divisions are problematic because most psalms shift from one type to another, for example, from lament to praise. Because identifying different basic types of psalms is somewhat helpful, I classify them as lament, thanksgiving, praise, penitential, and wisdom, following the lead of John C. Endres and Elizabeth Liebert, *A Retreat with the Psalms: Resources for Personal and Communal Prayer* (Mahwah, NJ: Paulist Press, 2001).

[7] A review of the Revised Common Lectionary at http://lectionarypage.net/ bears out this observation.

[8] https://www.pbs.org/wgbh/aia/part4/4h2927t.html, accessed 22 August 2020.

[9] https://www.theguardian.com/books/2015/apr/20/toni-morrison-race-relations-america-criminal-justice-system, accessed 21 August 2020.

[10] Kathryn Greene-McCreight, *Darkness Is My Only Companion: A Christian Response to Mental Illness* (Grand Rapids, MI: Brazos Press, 2006), 71.

The Rosary

To take a seat in the little side chapel, I had to make my way past a row of older women and a couple of men, heads bowed over their beads, murmuring rapidly and in unison, *"Sainte Marie, Mère de Dieu, priez pour nous pauvres pécheurs, maintenant et à l'heure de notre mort."* Holy Mary, Mother of God, pray for us sinners now and at the hour of our death. When the group finished their rosary, the leader looked over at me. I was silently contemplating the altar where the eucharist would be celebrated in a few minutes.

"Voulez-vous prendre votre tour, madame?" Would you like to take a turn?

I smiled and shook my head. Someone else took the lead, and the group's recitation went on.

Not only did I not have a rosary with me, if someone had lent me one, I wouldn't have known how to start praying it. I was visiting the parish church of La Nativité-de-la-Sainte-Vierge-d'Hochelaga[1] on a different spiritual quest: to see for the first time the church where my father had worshiped as a young man. In 1950, at the age of 18, he moved from his family's small subsistence farm near the Vermont border to an office job in Montréal. His faith connected him to his mother, who had devoted a few years to the novitiate before leaving the convent to be married. She died several years after my father left home; her rosary remained on display in my grandfather's house, never used, as far as I know, after her death.

Occasionally, I rode along with my father to Mass, which he attended faithfully before dinner every Saturday, as my lapsed-Presbyterian mother stayed home. And I learned the Hail Mary, the anchor prayer of the rosary, in a seventh-grade religious education class. But outside Mass, I never saw my father pray, never saw him pick up a rosary, never asked him about any conversations he may have had with God, Jesus, or Mary. He was an intensely private person, and my mother warned me to respect his boundaries. And then, halfway through his fifties, when I had barely entered my twenties, he died, leaving much of his interior life a mystery. In the gap between the faith in which he was raised and the one I came to as an adult lies the rosary.

✠ ✠ ✠

When I was ordained to the priesthood, a member of my sponsoring congregation gave me a rosary. It hangs on the wall of my study, near a wooden angel a friend brought back from Guatemala and a tiny icon I bought at Canterbury Cathedral. For well over a decade, the rosary simply dangled there as a reminder of a fellow Christian's kindness. In the process of writing this book, I finally took down the rosary to use it for its intended purpose. In doing so, I was reminded of how valuable it can be to have a physical object tethering me to the act of prayer.

The custom of praying certain sets of prayers while keeping count with some physical object dates to the early centuries of Christianity—and was certainly practiced in the first monasteries. In the Western Church, the Lord's Prayer was the most commonly repeated prayer; in the East, what became known as "the Jesus Prayer" ("Lord, Jesus Christ, have mercy on me, a sinner") predominated.[2] Medieval Western Europeans developed the practice of adding repetitions of the Hail Mary to the Lord's Prayer as well as meditating on various mysteries of the Christian faith (in the context of the rosary, "mystery" means a moment in the life of Jesus or Mary that reveals a deep truth of the Christian faith). Praying the rosary in this way became particularly important to the majority of Christians who could not read and did not have the leisure to memorize large portions of scripture, especially the psalter, as priests and literate nuns did. Instead of praying the Liturgy of the Hours (the equivalent of the Daily Office), the unlettered faithful, including lay brothers and sisters who cooked and cleaned to sustain their colleagues' life of prayer, would commune with Jesus and his mother through the rosary. Over the course of a day, a person praying a full rosary would meditate on 15 holy mysteries while reciting 150 Hail Marys. The latter number became significant as it corresponded to the 150 psalms that the literate choir monks and nuns repeatedly chanted through the Liturgy of the Hours.

During this time, the Order of Preachers made it their special mission to spread the rosary. Commonly called the Dominicans, the order's better-known members include Thomas Aquinas, Catherine of Siena, and Martin de Porres. According to tradition, the order's founder, Dominic, complained to Mary about his lack of success in combating Catharism (also known as Albigensianism), a heresy teaching that the universe is a battleground between good (spirit) and bad (matter). Mary instructed Dominic to pray the rosary while meditating and preaching on the mysteries of the faith; this became the foundation of his order's spirituality and the source of their strength in the campaign against Catharism. The Dominican rosary, as adapted over time, is still the predominant form of this prayer practice.

Before writing this chapter, I knew that centuries of Western Christians had relied on the rosary for their personal and corporate devotions. Because of my limited experience with the rosary, I talked about the practice with a practitioner close to home: my friend Clarke, also an Episcopal priest. Clarke became an Anglican as an undergraduate at the University of Toronto. His voice was such a beautiful addition to the university chorus that the director invited him to sing in the choir of St. Thomas's Anglican Church, one of the oldest Anglo-Catholic parishes in Canada. With no previous experience of Roman or Anglo-Catholic worship, Clarke would stare at the church's "enormous" statue of Mary and wonder, "What is this? What is going on here?" As he dared to ask other parishioners about the statue, they shared their Marian devotion, and he decided to buy a rosary. "But I didn't know how to do it!" he remembers now. All he knew was that somehow, people who prayed the rosary used the beads to count Hail Marys. Beyond that, though, "I didn't know the full secret handshake," he says. Clarke finally got over his embarrassment and asked an Anglo-Catholic friend to teach him. That was about twenty-five years ago, and now the rosary is virtually a daily practice for him.

At least two things have happened along the way to confirm Clarke in this practice. First, it seems that his rosary prayers have literally been answered, more than once. "At two key moments in my life," he says, "I decided that I was going to take the Hail Mary prayer at its word, and I was going to ask for Mary to intervene on my behalf, and my prayers came true. And there was every reason to believe that they would not." In those two moments, he realized that his beseeching Jesus's mother to "pray for us sinners now and at the hour of our death" was an effective and worthy prayer for a disciple of her son. Second, he realized that the Song of Mary, the *Magnificat*, which Episcopalians routinely recite or chant in the Daily Office, clearly states core truths about God's liberating love. Mary, to my friend, "bears the standard" for that liberation. And as he has found, passing time with her in prayer every day can be a way of ensuring that God's priorities become our own.

So what is the rosary, exactly? On a literal, physical level, it's a closed strand of beads arranged in five groups of ten, with a single bead separating each decade (or set of ten); from this closed strand hangs a tail composed of a crucifix, a single bead, a group of three beads, and another single bead. Rosaries can be fashioned by knotting a piece of string or stringing precious jewels on a chain of gold or silver. They can be worn as a bracelet or a ring with ten raised bumps. Ten fingers or toes can be used as a rosary. The objects are simply a mnemonic device to keep the person praying from losing their place in the cycle of prayers. The prayers themselves are the actual rosary. The word "rosary" comes from the Latin *rosarium*: a string of Our Fathers and Hail Marys imagined as a garland of roses, her signature flower, offered to the Mother of God. Giving Mary and Jesus the rosary-prayers is the verbal equivalent of handing them a bouquet of flowers.

The prayers—the Our Fathers and the Hail Marys—are meant to be a contemplative device: familiar words that bring the pray-er consciously into the presence of God and then free the mind to focus on contemplating the holy mysteries that are the heart of this practice. The words of the Our Father and Hail Mary are (or, with practice, become) so familiar that one needn't think them to say them. Rather, they become the soundscape inside which one turns one's mind to the mysteries.

Classical rosary practice uses fifteen mysteries.

✠ The five joyful mysteries come from the beginning of Jesus's earthly life:

> *The Annunciation (Luke 1:26-38)³;*
> *The Visitation (Luke 1:39-56);*
> *The Nativity (Matthew 1:18-25; Luke 2:6-20);*
> *The Presentation (Luke 2:22-39);*
> *The Finding of Jesus in the Temple (Luke 2:41-51).*

✠ The five sorrowful mysteries are drawn from Jesus's Passion:

> *The Agony in the Garden (Matthew 26:36-46;*
> *Mark 14:32-42; Luke 22:39-46);*

The Scourging at the Pillar (Matthew 27:26; Mark 15:15; Luke 23:18-22; John 19:1);

The Crowning with Thorns (Matthew 27:29-30; Mark 15:16-20; John 19:2-3);

The Carrying of the Cross (Luke 23:26-32; Matthew 27:31-32; Mark 15:21);

The Crucifixion (Luke 23:33-47; Matthew 27:33-54; Mark 15:22-39; John 19:17-37).

✪ The five glorious mysteries focus on the resurrection and post-Resurrection events:

The Resurrection (Matthew 28:1-10; Mark 16:1-18; Luke 24:1-49; John 20:1-29);

The Ascension (Luke 24:50-51; Acts 1:6-11);

The Descent of the Holy Spirit (Acts 2:1-41);

The Assumption of Mary;

The Crowning of Mary as the Queen of Heaven.

In 2002, Pope John Paul II added what he called five "luminous mysteries," drawn from Jesus's earthly ministry. In a letter explaining why he was adding these mysteries to the rosary, Pope John Paul II wrote, "Certainly the whole mystery of Christ is a mystery of light. He is the 'light of the world' (John 8:12). Yet this truth emerges in a special way during the years of his public life when he proclaims the Gospel of the Kingdom."[4] John Paul singled out these events as holy mysteries to contemplate:

Jesus's Baptism in the River Jordan (Matthew 3:13-17; Mark 1:9-11; Luke 3:21-22; John 1:29-34);

The Miracle at Cana (John 2:1-11);

The Proclamation of the Kingdom of God, with his call to conversion (Matthew 4:12-17; Mark 1:14-15; and throughout the Gospels);

The Transfiguration (Matthew 17:1-8; Mark 9:2-8; Luke 9:28-36);

The Institution of the Eucharist (Matthew 26:26-29; Mark 14:22-25; Luke 22:14-20; 1 Cor 11:23-26).

Meditating on these 15 or 20 mysteries shows that love for Jesus lies at the heart of this prayer. As we pray the rosary, Mary is our companion as we contemplate her son's life, death, and resurrection, much as she was God's partner in bringing him into the world, Jesus's first teacher, and an early witness to his resurrection.

All that being said, not everyone will feel comfortable praying the rosary. Some may stumble over the two mysteries that are not scripturally attested but come from Roman Catholic dogma: the assumption of Mary into heaven and her crowning as Queen of Heaven.[5] If that's you, you might choose to think of the assumption as the belief that Mary is present with the Triune God in heaven, as all disciples hope one day to be, and you might think of her crowning as an expression of what many Anglicans hold to be true, that as Jesus's mother, the God-bearer, she is first among the saints. Or you might leave out these two and repeat two of the other glorious mysteries instead.

Some non-Catholics might be reluctant to use the rosary because they think it means "praying to Mary" rather than to God. Indeed, all prayer is properly addressed to God rather than to any fallible human or other creature that can so easily become an idol. In praying the rosary, however, we are literally asking Jesus's mother to pray *for* us, to intercede for us, in much the same way as we regularly ask friends and fellow Christians, some of whom we might not know personally, to hold us in their prayers. I think of Mary as an elder sister in faith, whose love of God, care for her son, and obedience to the divine will I would do well to emulate. And so, the practice of talking with her, asking her to speak to the Son or his Father on my behalf, encourages me in my own discipleship.

✛ ✛ ✛

So how does one pray the rosary? There are several variations on the practice, as a quick internet search reveals. You may even have heard of "the Anglican rosary." This practice, developed in the late twentieth century, uses scripture passages and selections from the Book of Common Prayer and the Lord's Prayer, and in some cases, omitting the Marian prayers. As with the Roman Catholic practice of praying the rosary, the beads serve as a helpful mnemonic to keep the person praying on track. As such, in some areas, the practice is called "Anglican prayer beads" or simply "praying with beads."[6]

The method for praying the rosary that I outline here is simple; I learned it as I wrote this chapter.[7] While there are different sets of rosary prayers, the method I offer here is the traditional Roman Catholic one. If you prefer another variation, I encourage you to search online or talk with a trusted faith leader. If you adopt the rosary as a practice, eventually, you will be able to pray it in waiting rooms, in line at the post office, and in other spare moments. When starting out, though, it's best to find a quiet spot where you won't be disturbed for twenty minutes to half an hour or so.

✠ Start by making the sign of the cross and saying, "In the name of the Father, and of the Son, and of the Holy Spirit" (or if you prefer, "In the name of the one, holy, and undivided Trinity").

✠ Holding your rosary by the crucifix, say the Apostles' Creed.

✠ Holding the single bead immediately above the crucifix, say the Lord's Prayer.

✠ On each of the next three beads, pray one Hail Mary. You can ask God for the virtues of faith, hope, and love: one of these virtues on each of these three beads.

> *"Hail Mary, full of grace, the Lord is with you. Blessed are you among women, and blessed is the fruit of your womb, Jesus. Holy Mary, Mother of God, pray for us sinners now and at the hour of our death. Amen."*

✠ On the chain (or string) between the group of three beads and the next bead, pray the Glory Be: "Glory to the Father, and to the Son, and to the Holy Spirit [or, "Praise to the holy and undivided Trinity, one God"]; as it was in the beginning, is now, and will be forever. Amen."

✠ The bead above the group of three is where you start your first decade. You will pray one decade (one Our Father, ten Hail Marys, and one Glory Be) for each mystery.

Holding this bead, recall the first mystery you will be contemplating; thank God for it; and then pray one Our Father.

While it is possible to pray fifteen or twenty decades in one sitting, working your way through all the mysteries, that's not a common practice, nor is it advisable for a beginner who is settling into a new practice. More common practice is to pray five decades in one sitting, contemplating the joyful, sorrowful, glorious, or luminous mysteries.

✠ After praying the Our Father, move to the first group of ten beads in the circle. (Traditionally, this practice moves around the circle counter-clockwise, but you can also move clockwise. The direction doesn't matter.) On each bead, pray one Hail Mary, for a total of ten.

After praying one Hail Mary for each of the first ten beads, pray the Glory Be on the chain (or string) after the tenth bead.

✠ On the single bead above the ten beads on which you just prayed, start your next decade with the Lord's Prayer. Moving to the next set of ten beads, follow the pattern laid out above until you have prayed five decades.

✠ When you have prayed five decades (or however many you pray in that sitting), two concluding prayers traditionally follow.

> The Salve Regina, *or Hail Holy Queen: "Hail Holy Queen, Mother of Mercy, our Life, our Sweetness, and our hope. To you we cry, poor banished children of Eve. To you we send up*

our sighs, mourning and weeping in this vale of tears. Turn then most gracious advocate, your eyes of mercy toward us, and after this, our exile, show us, the blessed fruit of your womb, Jesus. O clement, O loving, O sweet Virgin Mary. Pray for us O Holy Mother of God, that we may be made worthy of the promises of Christ. Amen."

The final collect: "O God, whose only begotten Son, by His life, death, and resurrection, has purchased for us the rewards of eternal life, grant, we beseech You, that meditating upon these mysteries of the Most Holy Rosary of the Blessed Virgin Mary, we may imitate what they contain and obtain what they promise, through the same Christ Our Lord. Amen."

It's traditional to meditate on the joyful mysteries on Mondays and Saturdays, sorrowful mysteries on Tuesdays and Fridays, the glorious mysteries on Wednesdays and Sundays, and the luminous mysteries on Thursdays, but you are free to contemplate those that call you in any given day or season.[8]

Regardless of how many decades one prays in a session or which mysteries one contemplates, the idea is to sink into the prayers, to bask in God's love as manifested in the life of Jesus, to seek the grace to be his faithful disciple, and to request his mother's help in bringing God's loving power into your own life and into the world.

Questions to consider and things to try

✥ If you have never prayed the rosary, consider praying it daily or a few times a week, for a week to a month. Notice what feels natural or welcome, or uncomfortable or off-putting, about this form of prayer. Consider whether it might become a regular discipline for you or an occasional practice.

✥ If you grew up praying the rosary and still do, consider what gift the practice gives you.

✥ If you used to pray it, but stopped, recall: did you and the rosary (or you and Mary) part on good terms? Take a loving, non-judgmental look at your feelings about the practice.

✥ Find a partner with whom to pray the rosary, especially if the practice is new to you.

✥ If you would like to learn more about the rosary, this book is a good guide: William G. Storey, *The Complete Rosary: A Guide to Praying the Mysteries* (Chicago: Loyola Press, 2006).

✥ Research the difference between the Roman Catholic and Anglican traditions. Which variation appeals to you? Why?

✥ As part of the practice, some people make their own rosary beads, offering prayers throughout the creation process. If this interests you, search for some instructions and make your own set of beads.

Endnotes

[1] In English, the Nativity of the Blessed Virgin of Hochelaga. "Hochelaga" is one rendering of the Iroquoian name for the Indigenous commercial and gathering site where the city of Montréal now stands. Hochelaga is also the name of the working-class neighborhood that is home to this parish church.

[2] I discuss the Jesus Prayer in the chapter on silent prayers.

[3] Scriptural references are given for your information. It's not typical to read the Bible as part of praying the rosary. If you feel so led, when beginning to pray the rosary, you might review the passages outlining the mysteries that you will be contemplating, maybe reading one day and praying the next.

[4] Pope John Paul II, "Rosarium Virginis Mariae," II:21 (2002), http://www.vatican.va/content/john-paul-ii/en/apost_letters/2002/documents/hf_jp-ii_apl_20021016_rosarium-virginis-mariae.html, accessed 6 October 2020.

[5] Mary is sometimes identified with the "woman clothed with the sun, with the moon under her feet, and on her head a crown of twelve stars" in Revelation 12:1. That symbolic woman could be seen as Israel, the Church, or Mary, and perhaps as all three, and more. The figurative, apocalyptic language of Revelation resists easy interpretation or simple decoding of symbols.

[6] This practice is described in helpful detail in Nan Lewis Doerr and Virginia Stem Owens, *Praying With Beads: Daily Prayers for the Christian Year* (Grand Rapids, MI: Eerdmans, 2007).

[7] Many thanks to Fr. Richard Peers of the Church of England, Superior of the Sodality of Mary Mother of Priests, for teaching me over video conference to pray the rosary.

[8] Traditionally, the Glory Be is replaced during the Triduum as follows. On Maundy Thursday: "Christ was made obedient for us unto death." On Good Friday: "Christ was made obedient for us unto death, even to death on a cross." On Holy Saturday: "Christ was made obedient for us unto death, even to death on a cross. Therefore God also highly exalted him and gave him the name that is above every name" (Philippians 2:8-9; the language used will vary slightly in different communities praying the rosary).

The Intercession
of the Saints

In the spring of 2019, the news was filled with stories of misery at
the southern border of the United States. A combination of policies
required non-Mexican asylum seekers to remain in Mexico while
their immigration cases were adjudicated and strictly limited the
number of Mexican asylum seekers allowed to cross the border
daily, trapping spiraling numbers of refugees in border towns on
the southern side. From social media and Episcopal News Service
updates, I knew Episcopal dioceses were offering material, spiritual,
and legal support to these migrant neighbors. And, with a sabbatical
coming up, I wondered what more I could do beyond the prayers
and money I was offering and the calls and e-mails I sent my elected
officials. Sitting on my back porch, praying Morning Prayer, I heard
what may have been the Holy Spirit: "You could go." I called friends
in the Diocese of the Rio Grande in far-west Texas and asked if there
were ways I could be useful. There were.

So that autumn, I lived for three weeks in Ciudad Juárez, Mexico, just
across the river from El Paso. My friends in Texas connected me to a

Mexican Anglican priest who gave me a room in his church's refugee shelter. There, I lived with migrants from Cuba who had made their way across Nicaragua, El Salvador, Guatemala, and the entire length of Mexico to arrive in this border city and with Mexicans who had been deported after decades in the United States. I passed my days on the streets around the Paso del Norte binational bridge, where a tent city of asylum seekers had sprung up. That community of 200 or so families quickly enfolded me, calling me *Pastora* and sharing stories of the violence that had driven them from their homes and of the relatives waiting for them in *El Norte*. Beyond listening, I could do only a few things to show my support. Every day, I bought water and diapers for the community to share that day. I escorted people with minor injuries to the local clinic, and I found shoes for migrants whose footwear had worn out on their long treks north and blankets to shield them ever so slightly from the frigid desert nights.

And I prayed.

I prayed with the parents of sick children; with women who had lost track of their husbands after the U.S. government split them up in detention before denying their asylum claim and deporting them separately back to Mexico, and with families as they gathered the courage to request entry to the United States. Standing beside my friends at the Customs and Border Patrol checkpoint as they stated their need for asylum, I silently implored a host of saints to intercede, leaning especially hard on Óscar Romero, Joseph, and the Blessed Virgin Mary. Over and over, I repeated, *Holy Mary, Mother of God, pray for us sinners now and at the hour of our death.* Aware of the violence that daily sweeps Ciudad Juárez, sometimes I added, "And please, may that hour not come soon."

I had reason to believe Óscar Romero, at least, was listening. A few days into my stay, I had begun meditating on how he, the Roman Catholic archbishop of San Salvador, had spoken up for the people of El Salvador who were targeted by their country's U.S.-backed dictatorship. Archbishop Romero was murdered in 1980 as he celebrated Holy Eucharist, one day after he had exhorted Salvadoran soldiers to refuse to kill their own people, reminding them, "No soldier is obliged to obey an order contrary to the law of God." Remembering how he had been willing to suffer a martyr's death for defending innocent victims of political violence, I asked Archbishop Romero to help my migrant friends.

The following day, returning from a trip to the corner store to pick up a few necessities, I realized I had 150 pesos more than I had left the shelter with. I had counted my money carefully before leaving, and both the cashier and I had checked to make sure I received the correct change. "Well, I must have miscounted," I shrugged. But the next morning, I gave a bus driver 200 pesos to cover the 64-peso fare for eight shelter residents. After the bus had pulled away, I realized the conductor had given me back 276 pesos. The 200-peso note was not my original bill, and the 76 pesos was a random number. Grabbing a friend's hand to get her attention, I told her how these strange windfalls had come so soon after asking Archbishop Romero to intercede for our asylum-seeking friends. With her as my witness, I promised to spend the extra pesos on them. (I also said a prayer for the bus driver, hoping he wouldn't be found short at the end of the day. Knowing the chaotic nature of fare collection on Juárez's overstuffed buses, I trusted he would not.)

I'm not saying Christians should treat the saints who have gone on to glory as our personal cash machine or even as a benevolent uncle or grandma who likes to slip us a twenty every once in a while. The saints are not magical spirits bound to do our bidding; not every Saint Joseph statue buried upside down in a front yard leads to a quick house sale, and not every appeal to Saint Anthony results in a lost object being found. (I know this from experience.) Even our most fervent entreaties don't turn out the way we desire one hundred percent of the time. I offered Hail Marys on each trip to a border checkpoint. Some of the asylum-seekers I accompanied gained entry at least long enough to make a formal request for protection, and some texted later to say they had landed safely in new American homes, but many others were turned away.

But calling on the saints for help is a faithful and time-honored practice of the church. And given that Christians are disciples of the man who fed crowds of thousands with a few loaves and a couple of fish, maybe I shouldn't have been surprised that appealing for help to our brother Óscar—murdered while celebrating Mass—apparently yielded cash to buy water for refugees waiting on sidewalks under a desert sun.

The communion of saints is a broad fellowship. It includes everyone, living and dead, who has been baptized into Jesus Christ's Body, so that every Christian is, theologically speaking, a saint: a person in and through whom the Holy Spirit moves and works. Beyond this inclusive definition, the church singles out certain departed members of this communion, from Jesus's time to the present day, as saints whose lives offer an especially powerful witness to the gospel. The Episcopal Church's prayer for the Feast of All Saints expresses this dual reality of including all while elevating some. It acknowledges that all Christians are "knit together…in one communion and fellowship in the mystical body of …Christ our Lord," while also asking that God would "give us grace so to follow your blessed saints in all virtuous and godly living, that we may come to those ineffable joys that you have prepared for those who truly love you" (The Book of Common Prayer, 245). Some especially "blessed saints" are remembered in liturgical calendars, lifted up and celebrated on what the church calls their "feast day" (usually observed on the date of their death, their entrance into eternal life).[1]

In theological terms, asking a departed saint to intercede for me, or one of my prayer intentions, is substantively the same as asking a living friend to do so.[2] It's not necessarily the same physical experience. A living friend can assure me, out loud or in writing, that they will pray for me. They can send a text out of the blue, call me up, or post to my social media to remind me that they're doing so. And they can rejoice with me when the healing or other good I desired happens, and mourn with me, or help me discern next steps, when the answer to my prayer appears to be "no." Many Christians don't receive that kind of feedback from saints who have passed on. Many do receive it, however, through a palpable sense of their presence with us and sometimes through experiences like my windfalls in Ciudad Juárez.

And so we continue to ask our dead siblings in Christ for help, just as we appeal to the living. Asking for the intercession of the saints, living and dead, highlights two features of Christian prayer: first, that when we pray, often we are requesting something, seeking to channel divine power toward some desired (and, we hope, holy) purpose; and second, that we are never united with God alone. By virtue of our baptism, we are always in the company of billions who have also been made one with Jesus Christ through the paschal mystery: the reality that Jesus Christ suffered, died, and rose again to unite human beings to God and each other. By asking others to pray with and for us, we acknowledge our unity, and we devote our combined efforts to what we hope are God's purposes. Together, we tap into that power that Jesus told his disciples would flow through us.

Christians have come together in this way from our earliest days. The third-century Egyptian theologian Origen assured the church that "these pray along with those who genuinely pray: not only the high priest [Jesus Christ] but also the angels…and also the souls of the saints already at rest."[3] His contemporary, Cyprian of Carthage, explicitly pointed to love as the motivator for prayer in this life and the next. In a time and place where Christians were being martyred, he wrote to an exiled friend, "Let us remember one another in concord and unanimity. Let us on both sides [of death] always pray for one another. Let us relieve burdens and afflictions by mutual love, that if one of us…shall go hence the first, our love may continue in the presence of the Lord, and our prayers for our brethren and sisters not cease in the presence of the Father's mercy."[4] A century and a half later, after Christianity had become the official religion of the Roman Empire, Augustine of Hippo reminded the faithful that "Christians pay religious honor to the memory of the martyrs," not only to benefit from their prayers but also "to excite us to imitate them."[5] For many Christians of African, Asian, or Indigenous American origins, an especially strong sense of their ancestors' love, support, and help is a theologically and culturally faithful expression of the church's belief in community that transcends planes of being.

Intercessory prayer reminds us that we have friends and extended family beyond the people we can see, text, or phone. It points to the ways in which Christians' lives have witnessed to God's love, spurring us to cultivate those virtues in ourselves. And it reminds us of the power we share, the divine power that Jesus Christ entrusted to his disciples through the Holy Spirit.

As discussed in this book's chapter on the rosary, some Christians who are not Roman Catholic feel uncomfortable asking departed saints to intercede for them. Debates on this subject raged through the Reformation for two main reasons. First, it seemed to Protestants that the Roman Catholic practice of praying to the saints had developed to the point where Christians worshiped human beings rather than the Triune God. Second, many feared that appealing to the intercession of the saints would downplay Jesus Christ's role as what the New Testament's First Letter to Timothy calls our "one Mediator." The Church of England's 39 Articles of Religion of 1562 dismissed "invocation of saints" along with Purgatory and the "worship" or "adoration" of images as "a fond thing vainly invented."[6] When thinking about the intercession of the saints, it's important to remember the difference between worshiping and praying to Jesus Christ as our one Mediator, who reconciled all humanity to God and each other and asking another human being (in this life or the next) to pray for us.

The saints who have passed on to the next realm can do as much to build up our faith and strengthen us for this earthly pilgrimage as our friends who are still breathing. Remembering Mary's openness to

God's liberating creativity, I can ask her to help my efforts to gain holy freedom, a new beginning, for myself or others. Joseph, her spouse, is invoked as a defender of children, families, and workers; the statue of him that stands outside my front door reminds me to attend to his priorities, which, in the end, are God's too. Óscar Romero spoke the truth and protected the poor when powerful people wanted him to be silent and enjoy a comfortable episcopate; these are excellent virtues for a white, middle-class priest like me to ask God's help in emulating. And since I believe that these three saints, and countless others, are currently in God's presence, praising our Lord and intervening on behalf of God's purposes in the world, I find it helpful consciously to join my efforts to theirs and to ask for their help in revealing divine love.

The intercession of the saints is not simply something Christians ask the dead to do for the living. All the baptized are members of the communion of saints, and so whenever we pray, we are called to pray for each other. Intercessory prayer has been part of celebrations of the eucharist and daily prayer services from as far back as written sources go because praying for the needs of the assembled people and their neighbors and the world has always been part of the church's ministry. The catechism in the Book of Common Prayer explicitly mentions prayer in its definition of the communion of saints as "the whole family of God, the living and the dead, those whom we love and those whom we hurt, bound together in Christ by sacrament, prayer, and praise."[7]

These words remind us that we are in communion with those whom we love and those whom we hurt—and, by implication, those who have hurt us, too. This includes the asylum-seekers I met in Ciudad Juárez and immediately loved, and those whose stories, rightly or wrongly, made me wonder if they had committed some of the crimes they described; the Customs and Border Patrol agents I found helpful, and those who seemed to delight in turning people away; the *gringa* priest who sojourned a few weeks with suffering Mexican and Central American neighbors and then returned to her comfortable life across the river; the politicians who make the laws immigration officials have to enforce. All of us are created, loved, and sustained by God; all of us who claim the name Christian are knit together into one Body. All of us can be channels of divine power, and all of us can spur each other to reflect more and more of God's glory—to become, more fully, God's saints.

Questions to consider and things to try

✠ On All Saints' Day (November 1), thank God for all the saints, those who have died and for those who are still alive, those you have learned about and those you have known personally. On this day, do something to honor a saint who is still here on earth (perhaps write them a note, if appropriate, to express your appreciation). On All Souls' Day (November 2; sometimes called "The Day of the Dead"), thank God for the saints commemorated by the church. Consider doing something to honor a saint who has passed on (such as an act of service or a gift in their memory).

✠ Leaf through *Lesser Feasts and Fasts*,[8] the Episcopal Church's supplemental liturgical calendar that celebrates saints as diverse as Thomas Aquinas, Harriet Tubman, and Florence Li Tim-Oi. Notice who catches your attention and who demonstrates virtues you would like to cultivate. Thank God for those saints and their example. When you are in a situation where their particular gifts could help, ask them to pray with you for whatever your intention is. If you develop a particular relationship with one or two saints, find a way to celebrate their feast day.

✠ Participate in "Lent Madness," an annual offering of Forward Movement, in which 32 saints are placed in single-elimination brackets, with members of the public voting daily, online, for one of each pair to advance. Saints may progress to the round of Saintly Sixteen, Elate Eight, and Faithful Four, until one receives the Golden Halo. It's a fun and instructive devotion for individuals, households, and whole congregations.[9]

✠ Consciously practice intercessory prayer. Ask people how, specifically, you may pray for them. Ask them about their needs and desires. Ask other people to pray for you. If there's someone in your life—a family member, a colleague, or a public figure—who consistently gets under your skin or with whom you're in such conflict that you can't imagine praying for them, consider asking someone else to do so on your behalf. Does knowing someone else is praying for that person, over time, change anything about how you see them?

Endnotes

[1] The feast days of some saints, like the original apostles, Mary Magdalene and Mary the mother of Jesus, are considered "major holy days" in the liturgical calendar (The Book of Common Prayer, 31-33), while many other saints are remembered on "lesser feasts" that are typically less widely observed.

[2] "Intention" in devotional language simply means the aim or purpose for which one is praying or asking someone else to pray.

[3] Origen, "On Prayer," VI, trans. William A. Curtis, http://www.tertullian.org/fathers/origen_on_prayer_02_text.htm, accessed 12 December 2020.

[4] Cyprian of Carthage, Epistle 56, https://www.newadvent.org/fathers/050656.htm, accessed 12 December 2020.

[5] Augustine, "Against Faustus the Manichean," 21, https://www.newadvent.org/fathers/140620.htm, accessed 12 December 2020.

[6] https://www.churchofengland.org/prayer-and-worship/worship-texts-and-resources/book-common-prayer/articles-religion, accessed 12 December 2020. The Articles of Religion were adopted by the Episcopal Church in 1801, after it was constituted as an independent church; they are found among the historical documents at the back of the Book of Common Prayer.

[7] The Book of Common Prayer 1979, 862.

[8] *Lesser Feasts and Fasts 2018* can be bought in printed form, or can be consulted or downloaded here: https://extranet.generalconvention.org/staff/files/download/21034, accessed 18 March 2021.

[9] https://www.lentmadness.org/about/

Ignatian Prayer

I settled into my rocking chair and opened the Bible to the Sermon on the Mount.

"Blessed are the poor in spirit," I heard Jesus say, "for theirs is the kingdom of heaven." Pausing to close my eyes for a moment, I saw myself standing with the other disciples around our seated Teacher. We all wondered what might come next. He continued, "Blessed are those who mourn, for they will be comforted. Blessed are the meek, for they will inherit the earth. Blessed are those who hunger and thirst for righteousness, for they will be filled. Blessed are the merciful, for they will receive mercy."

Those first disciples were so lucky, I thought. (*Besides being jailed, tortured, and executed,* I reminded myself. *OK, fair point,* I answered back.) But still: they got to hear Jesus preach. In the flesh. What a moment that would have been. What I wouldn't give to stand next to Jesus.

And then, there he was: peeking his head around the doorframe, a wide smile crinkling the corners of his warm brown eyes. Two long steps brought him next to my chair, where he stood looking down at me. *Do I give him my seat?* I wondered. But he plopped himself down on the floor, cross-legged. Closing my eyes again, I repeated his beatitudes to myself.

"Blessed are the pure in heart, for they will see God."

I'm not particularly pure in heart. Opening one eye, I saw Jesus looking up at me, still smiling. But God is good, and has a sense of humor, and chose this moment to remind me that Jesus is, in fact, with me.

I learned this imaginative way of praying from a sixteenth-century Basque priest who has become one of my closest companions.

Saint Ignatius of Loyola summarized his approach to life in two statements. First, that "human beings are created to praise, reverence, and serve God our Lord, and by means of this to save their souls"; and second, that everything in the world was created by God and can be a pathway to knowing and serving God.[1]

I can sum up what Ignatius has taught me in one reminder and one admonition: God loves you; pay attention.

Until he was about thirty, Ignatius thought his life's purpose was to make a name for himself in the military (and unofficially, as a man beloved by women—as many women as possible). But in 1521, as French forces attacked the fortress of Pamplona that Ignatius and his fellow soldiers were defending, he lost track of the line between courage and recklessness. Even after it became clear that Spanish resistance was futile, Ignatius convinced his commander to hold out. His powers of persuasion needlessly endangered lives on both sides and, as it turned out, ended Ignatius's military career. As he patrolled the ramparts, a French cannonball shattered his leg.

Recuperating at his elder brother's home, Ignatius asked for something to read. As he later wrote in his autobiography, he was hoping for some of the "worldly books of fiction, commonly labeled chivalry" that he had always enjoyed.[2] But apparently, there were no such books in the house. Instead, his brother's wife, Magdalena, brought him a book narrating the life of Christ and one recounting the lives of noted saints like Francis and Dominic. Books were less readily available then, and it may be that no one in his brother's household shared Ignatius's taste in literature. But I've always wondered if his sister-in-law, an observant Christian who had brought devotional books with her when she moved into her marital home, seized the chance to try to turn Ignatius from a path of which she disapproved. "But these books are all I have, brother," I imagine her saying, innocently spreading her hands as she left Ignatius to grumble.

If conversion was Magdalena's plan, it worked. Ignatius tumbled into the stories of Jesus and the lives of some of his most faithful followers, finding inspiration for a new life of his own. He rose from his sickbed, ready to devote to God the zeal he had formerly poured into military service. He eventually discerned two purposes for himself and the religious order he founded, the Society of Jesus (members of which are called Jesuits): to help others and to seek God in all things.

Today, there are Jesuit medical doctors, screenwriters, and astronomers, as well as parish priests, teachers, and writers. Calling themselves "contemplatives in action," Jesuits keep Ignatius's imaginative, inquiring approach to prayer at the heart of everything they do. The three main practices of Ignatian prayer are all characterized by disciplined self-reflection, awareness of the movement both of the Holy Spirit and of more destructive forces in the world, and the conviction that God is present with us in all circumstances and will use all things—including our feelings, experiences, and imaginations—to draw us closer. We'll explore each of these practices below.

✝ ✝ ✝

Imaginative prayer, or "Ignatian contemplation," invites us to bring our whole selves—our experiences, thoughts, feelings, senses—into a reverent, expectant encounter with scripture. Father James Martin, a well-known Jesuit writer, says that this method of prayer "asks you to enter into Bible stories imaginatively and accept that God can work through your imagination to help you see things in fresh ways."[3] The idea is not to try to understand the passage in a historical context nor to compare different versions of the same story for interesting similarities and differences (although these can be fruitful ways to engage with scripture). Rather, you're reading to hear Jesus's word for you, a sinner whom God loves and with whom God desires a closer relationship, in whatever circumstances you find yourself.

So, start by finding a passage to read—whether it's assigned by the daily or weekly lectionary, is appropriate to the season, is an old favorite, or just catches your interest that day.[4] It's probably most helpful to pray with a piece of scripture that has a strong storyline, such as an event from the life of Jesus, Moses, or another person, or with a piece of poetry in which it's easy to place yourself, like a psalm. This method of prayer probably won't be as effective with a text that's, say, more legal or descriptive in nature, like the books of Deuteronomy or Leviticus (but if you find a piece in either or both of those books that work for you, go with it).

If you pray with a biblical story that features Jesus, don't be surprised to find yourself encountering him directly, as I did when he peered around the doorframe into the room where I sat with the beatitudes. You might feel the boat lurch as he stands up to still the storm while you cower, terrified, on the floor. You might feel sheepish, defensive, or amused as you hear him ask, "Why are you afraid?" You might feel deeply curious, and maybe frightened, as you ponder who this is, who calms the waves with a voice that only God should be able to summon, but whose breath, as he wakes, smells all too human. And while you are feeling all these things, at any moment, Jesus might turn to you and smile. So be open to meeting him, trusting that you are safe and loved as you seek to pass some time in his company.

To practice imaginative prayer, sit somewhere you feel comfortable and won't be disturbed for twenty to thirty minutes. Read your Bible passage once through to get the gist of what happens in it. Then read it again once or twice, sinking into the scene. Engage your senses. If, for example, you read the story of Jesus calming the storm, imagine what the wind and the disciples and Jesus sound like, what the water smells like, what the sway and bounce of the boat feel like, and what, if anything, you can see through the tempest.[5] With whom do you identify? Which utterances resonate the most with you? "Do you not care that we are perishing?" "Peace! Be still!" "Why are you afraid?" "Who, then, is this?"

See where your interaction with the text takes you; what word of encouragement or warning it might have for you. Consider taking a few notes to reflect on later. As your time of prayer comes to an end, thank God for your time together and for any insights you may have gained, and ask God to help you remember the gifts this time gave you.

It's important to note that Ignatius was not the only person to pray with scripture, placing himself in the stories and reading his own life through a biblical lens. God's people have always prayed with and through the stories of our faith, drawing connections between the past and their present, remembering God's promises and trusting they would be fulfilled or proclaiming that they had. Mary is often cast as a new Eve, birthing a new beginning for all humanity; Jesus feeding the five thousand recalls God's gift of manna to the liberated Israelites; on the day of Pentecost, Peter proclaims that the day of the Lord promised by the prophet Joel has arrived.

In the United States, enslaved people of African descent didn't need Ignatius, or any European, to teach them how to imagine themselves and their community into the scriptural story, most especially the story of the Exodus.

When Israel was in Egypt's land, let my people go; oppressed so hard they could not stand, let my people go...

He delivered Daniel from the lion's den, an' Jonah from the belly of the whale; An' the Hebrew children from the fiery furnace, An' why not every man.

Steal away, steal away, steal away to Jesus! Steal away, steal away home, I ain't got long to stay here! Tombstones are bursting, poor sinner stands a-trembling; the trumpet sounds within my soul, I ain't got long to stay here.[6]

Spirituals like "Go Down, Moses," "Didn't My Lord Deliver Daniel," and "Steal Away," expressed enslaved people's faith that God who had conquered Pharaoh, shut the mouths of Nebuchadnezzar's lions, and raised Jesus after his state-approved lynching, would not let slavery continue forever—and their hope that freedom would come soon. These songs also served as signals that a friend or family member planned to "steal away" soon or that a conductor on the Underground Railroad like Harriet Tubman (known as Moses) was in the neighborhood to help others liberate themselves as she had done. The people who wrote and sang these songs knew that scripture was a living Word, and they used their imaginations to offer fervent prayers for themselves and their loved ones, and to affirm that those who held them in slavery would not escape God's judgment. Today, we can offer similar hopeful prayers, whether for ourselves or for neighbors whose lives are still being stolen from them, and we can heed the same call to repent and amend our lives.

✝ ✝ ✝

The second type of prayer for which Ignatius of Loyola is known is the examen, or examination of consciousness: a systematic review of the day's events, in the service of better self-understanding, a closer relationship to God, and greater skill in discerning God's will.[7] Jesuits normally pray the examen twice a day, at noon and at the end of the day. The rest of us can do the examen at any convenient time, usually once a day, and most commonly toward the end of the day (before dinner or before bed). It consists of five steps, which I shorthand as "Hello," "Thank you," "Take a look," "Sorry," "Help." It may help to keep a journal handy and take a few notes as you slowly move through these steps.

✣ *Hello*: Settle in, taking a moment to realize you are in God's presence and to ask for divine guidance as you review the day (or the previous several hours, if you do the examen twice a day).

✣ *Thank you*: Start by thanking God for two or three good things that happened in your day, for which you are particularly grateful. As Ignatius would say, savor these things as if they were a treat. (You may also have things on your mind that you regret. Ignore them for now; you'll talk to God about them in a few minutes.) Thank God for the people who facilitated these things, like a friend who called you; the pharmacist who administered your flu shot; the mail carrier who delivered good news.

✣ *Take a look:* Now, slowly review your day. Notice where you experienced God's presence: maybe in a small miracle, like a flower or birdsong; maybe in conversation with an old friend who may know you even better than you know yourself. As you look back over the day, consider: When did you serve as a channel for God's love? When did you experience love? What were those graced moments like? What happened in them? How did you feel?

✙ *Sorry*: As you look back over your day, you probably notice moments where you sinned, did something you regretted, or missed an opportunity to be kind. Now is the time to ask God's forgiveness and God's help to be more responsive tomorrow. It's also the time to notice those moments when you felt sorrowful as you experienced sin and broken relationships in the world (for example, in reading the news). After reflecting on your own sins and asking God's forgiveness, consider whether God might be calling you to any further action, such as apologizing and offering amends to a person you have hurt, doing something to accompany or assist someone in pain or need, or taking action to disrupt an ongoing societal sin like institutional racism.

Be kind to yourself, remembering that you won't receive all the answers you seek or be completely transformed overnight. The examen is meant to make you more aware and responsive to the Holy Spirit and more skilled at resisting sin's lures over time.

✙ *Help*: After you've reviewed the things for which you're grateful, those moments where you saw God's handiwork especially vividly, and those moments where you and the communities you are a part of fell short, it's time to close the book on the day (or half of the day) that is past. The next step is to ask God's grace for tomorrow. You can be specific: if you need a particular virtue or gift (such as kindness or clarity), ask for it by name. If you don't know what you need, tell God that. Be as open and honest as you can about how you are feeling and what you need. And then finish the examen by thanking God again.

If you keep notes on your examen, over time, you will notice the characteristic movements in your life of what Ignatius called the "good spirit," leading you in Christ's path, and of the "bad spirit," often manifested as patterns of temptation, characteristic sins, unhelpful habits, and destructive emotional patterns that get in the way of your following Jesus. Paying attention to these patterns will increase your skill at following the good spirit and resisting the bad spirit—or rebuking it in the name of Jesus. If you're tempted to become discouraged by the bad spirit's activity in your life, remember: Christians trust that the Holy Spirit is infinitely more powerful than sin, evil, and even death. The fact that you are praying means you are already responding to the divine call. Keep responding, and God will guide you.

A third practice of Ignatian prayer is the Spiritual Exercises. The Exercises grew out of Ignatius's own experience as he prayed with scripture, examined his conscience, and helped others do the same. Over time, he gathered his insights, the techniques of imaginative prayer and examen, and instructions for fellow Jesuits and others who would serve as directors into a book called "The Spiritual Exercises." This book is a manual for directors rather than a text one would read through or pray from without guidance. Working with a spiritual director is a key part of the Exercises. Exercitants (that's the technical term) often experience strong emotional responses in making the Exercises, and it's important to have a companion along the way for support and help in discernment.

There are two main ways of making the Spiritual Exercises of St. Ignatius: a thirty-day stay at a retreat house or a "retreat in everyday life" over about nine months, praying for about an hour a day, and meeting for an hour a week with a director.[8] The latter format is known as "the Nineteenth Annotation," for the simple reason that Ignatius describes this process in the nineteenth note of his guidebook to the Exercises. In either case, the purpose of the Exercises is the same: "To overcome oneself, and to order one's life, without reaching a decision through some disordered affection."[9] In other words, to get to know ourselves as sinners beloved by God and to learn to discern the difference between the prompting of the Holy Spirit and the urgings of the spirits that do not have our best interests at heart. As we grow in this awareness and skill, we will be less likely to put any of God's creatures (like money, a job, or some form of power over others) at the center of our lives where only God belongs. And we will deepen our relationship with Jesus Christ in order better to love God, our neighbor, and ourselves through the faithful action that is the fruit of time passed consciously in the divine presence.

Whether one makes a thirty-day retreat or the Nineteenth Annotation, the Exercises are divided into four "Weeks." These Weeks don't necessarily correspond to chronological weeks but rather to different experiences or movements.

- ✛ Before beginning Week 1, we take some time to reflect on God's boundless love for us and all creation. We are reassured that we have nothing to fear in approaching God.

- ✛ In Week 1, we reflect on our limited response to God's love—on our sinfulness—and pray for the grace to embrace ourselves as sinners beloved and redeemed by God.

- ✛ In Week 2, we reflect on Jesus's call to be his disciples. We pray to know him better so that we can love and follow him better in whatever way we are called to.

- ✛ In Week 3, we reflect on Jesus's suffering and death.

- ✛ In Week 4, we walk with him through his resurrection and savor the consolation of his victory over death.

Through these four weeks, the exercitant will experience what Ignatius called "consolation"—an awareness of God's loving presence—and "desolation"—a sense of God's apparent absence even though Christians affirm God is always near to us. Consolations are always to be savored, and the memories of them should be stored up to recall during those desolate moments that all of us experience at some point. The director is present, in part, to rejoice with the exercitant in moments of consolation and to encourage them in desolation. Sometimes, they help the exercitant recognize that apparent desolation is, in fact, a sign of God's presence; the classic example is when the exercitant is overcome by an awareness of their own sin, which births a desire to amend their life. Learning the characteristic ways in which one is prone to deceiving oneself and asking God's help to change is a common benefit of making the Exercises.

The Exercises, like Ignatian prayer in general, are not for everyone. Making them requires a significant commitment of time and energy and a financial commitment in compensating the director. For that matter, the imaginative and emotional approach that came intuitively to Ignatius doesn't suit everyone. But if Ignatius's approach resonates with you, and if you devote time to self-examination in the company of Jesus, engaging your whole mind, body, and soul in the process, you will very likely meet Jesus anew and be changed.

Questions to consider and things to try

✛ Practice the examen, Ignatian contemplation, or both, daily for a month. If finding time for Ignatian contemplation daily is a struggle, try it once or twice a week (maybe using the gospel lesson from the previous or upcoming Sunday). Keep notes about your experiences. At the end of each week, review your notes from those seven days, and at the end of the month, review again what you wrote over the entire period. Do you notice any patterns, moments when something changed, or reassurances, challenges, or invitations you received? Ask God for help in discerning what those might mean.

✛ Invite a trusted friend to do this practice, too. Each week, discuss what the previous week's prayers showed you about your relationship with God, your neighbor, and yourself.

✛ Read *Jesus: A Pilgrimage* by James Martin, SJ, (New York: Harper One, 2016) for a personal introduction to imaginative prayer and the examen.

✛ If there is a Jesuit parish or retreat house near you, or if a Jesuit community farther away offers retreats by video conference, consider making an individual guided retreat or joining a group retreat. The retreat might last a day, a weekend, or (a common practice) eight days.

✛ If you have been persisting in prayer for some time, and especially if you have worked with a spiritual director (about which I say more in its own chapter), consider whether you might benefit from making the Spiritual Exercises. You could start by raising the possibility with your director; peruse the websites of retreat houses that offer the Exercises, to see if what they offer appeals to you, and/or consult with a director who leads people through the Exercises.

Endnotes

1 "The Spiritual Exercises" 23, in Ignatius of Loyola, *Ignatius of Loyola: Spiritual Exercises and Selected Works,* trans. and ed. George E. Ganss, sj (Mahwah, NJ: Paulist Press, 1991).

2 "The Autobiography" 1:5, in *Ignatius of Loyola,* trans. and ed. George E. Ganss, sj.

3 James Martin, sj, Jesus: *A Pilgrimage,* (New York: Harper One, 2014), 10.

4 Sunday lectionary readings can be found at http://lectionarypage.net/ and the daily lectionary at http://lectionarypage.net/#dailylectio.

5 Mark 4:35-41, Matthew 8:23-27, Luke 8:22-25.

6 These lyrics are from well-known spirituals. A good source for additional spirituals is *Lift Every Voice and Sing II: An African American Hymnal* (New York: Church Publishing Incorporated, 1993).

7 Ignatius wrote in Spanish, in which the word *conciencia* signifies both the English "consciousness" and "conscience." So the examen can be translated as either "examination of consciousness," "examination of conscience," or both.

8 Although Ignatius's original Spanish *hacer* could be translated either "to make" or "to do," it is traditional, in English, to refer to "making" the Exercises rather than "doing" them.

9 "The Spiritual Exercises" 21, in *Ignatius of Loyola,* trans. and ed. George E. Ganss, sj.

Lectio Divina

The news never got better. Mostly, it got worse. But I could hardly tear myself away. Not every night, but more and more often as the coronavirus pandemic wore on, I caught myself at it again: doomscrolling. (The word's origins predate the pandemic by a couple of years, but it gained new relevance in 2020.) Clutching my smartphone in one hand, my other index finger flicking away, tumbling deeper and deeper down the rabbit hole of bad news, absorbing little of what I read, consoling myself with…what, exactly? The fact that the world still turned? That none of the misfortune, folly, and sin that filled the headlines had yet caused it to implode or spin out of orbit? Cold, scant comfort.

I knew doomscrolling was a bad idea. I never succumbed without rolling my eyes at my apparent expectation that somehow, I would be able to get to sleep after these mad scrambles across graphs depicting spiking COVID rates and unemployment claims, photos of families lined up at food pantries, and headlines screaming the United States president's refusal to concede his electoral defeat and leave office gracefully.

These interactions with the written word didn't deserve to be dignified by the term "reading." They yielded little information, no pleasure, and only occasional appreciation for the skills of the journalists who had produced the items my fingers flicked over. To find my footing again, I needed to fall into a different kind of reading, to lose myself in different words. I needed to slow down, chew over some news that was actually good. To pass some time in the company, not of my own anxiety, grief, and rage, but of the One who loves the world too fiercely ever to abandon any of its inhabitants. I needed to slow down and immerse myself, again, in the words that promise healing for the ill and grief-stricken, liberation for captives, forgiveness for the repentant. I needed to hear divine murmurings of love again, nudging me to love.

Lectio divina ("holy reading" in Latin) invites us into a particular, intimate relationship with the words of scripture—a relationship that runs contrary to most of the ways we typically read. When I open the Bible to pray in this way, I'm not reading for information, not scanning to see if there's anything useful in a page, not trying to get through as much of the book as possible in the time available, not evaluating whether I agree or take issue with the author's point of view. Even if I'm an absolute newcomer to Christianity, I'm not reading to see how the story turns out. Instead, I'm reading a short passage slowly, accepting God's invitation to watch and listen for what scripture might have to say to me in this particular moment, in whatever circumstances I find myself—pandemic or prosperity, transition or stability, worry or contentment. I'm moving deliberately, trusting that God is present, reaching out to me, and always ready for me to reach back. I'm not alone on my sofa, stress-munching potato chips or clenching my jaw obliviously. I'm enjoying a leisurely meal with a friend whose company turns the simplest of dishes into a feast.

Lectio divina as we know it comes from the Benedictine monastic tradition, beginning in sixth-century Italy. Saint Benedict offered a Rule (his instructions for how monks were to live) that specified brothers "should have specified periods for manual labor as well as for prayerful reading."[1] The practice's roots, however, extend even farther back in time and geographically south to Africa. Origen of Alexandria (in Egypt), a third-century biblical scholar and theologian, taught that the resurrected Jesus Christ was present in scripture and that Christians could meet him by reading the Bible—or more likely in Origen's time, by hearing it read. Ambrose, the fourth-century bishop of Milan, was introduced to this idea from Origen's writings, and he taught the practice of prayerful reading to his student Augustine, the future theologian and bishop of Hippo (in current-day Algeria).

From the beginning, these theologians and teachers of prayer used gastronomic metaphors for the practice of meditating on scripture. In his instructions to clergy on how to live out their vocation, Ambrose wrote, "The divine scriptures are the feast of wisdom, and the single books the various dishes."[2] In his *Confessions*, Augustine recalled that as he got to know Ambrose, he realized "the encouragement [Ambrose] received in times of difficulty, [and] what exquisite delights he savored in his secret mouth, the mouth of his heart, as he chewed the bread of your word."[3] Following Ambrose's example of ruminating over God's word, Augustine later experienced these gifts for himself.

Augustine's translator, Maria Boulding, osb, noted that what she called Ambrose and Augustine's "gastronomic metaphors" for reading were common until at least the end of the medieval period.[4] For centuries, Boulding wrote, "the reading of scripture was understood as an activity involving the whole person, physical as well as mental and spiritual." Although today you or I might speak of "devouring" a book or perhaps refer to a plot twist as "delicious," we don't commonly think of reading as a gustatory, let alone whole-body, activity.

But consider the physical effects a story can have. It can make your heart race with anger, excitement, or anticipation. It can make you gasp with surprise, laugh uproariously, or weep with grief. This can even be true on the umpteenth experience of a book: I have read

Anne of Green Gables every year since I was seven or eight, and every time, I sob when Anne's adopted parent Matthew dies and suck my teeth with irritation at Lucy Maud Montgomery's insulting portrayal of a French-speaking Canadian. If we don't fall prey to the false dichotomy between mind (or spirit) and body, it's easier to see that our whole self, our whole person, can be immersed in reading. The stories that draw us in shape us. That's why literature can be described as "edifying," and that's why the Acts of the Apostles remembers Paul referring to the gospel as "a message that is able to build you up."[5]

Sometimes, the fact that a story might be edifying, or somehow good for us, makes us worry that it will be boring, something to plod through, not pleasurable. Think, though, of the various foods you need to regenerate, stay healthy, and enjoy life as the embodied creature you are; of the foods that give you a thrill of sheer pleasure or that make you shake your head in amazement at a cook's skill or ingenuity; of the dishes that, however they may have tasted, expressed someone's care and concern for you. Pleasure and nurture are not at odds in the realm of food, nor are they at odds in the practice of prayer. Augustine—never one to shy away from sensual metaphors for human relations with God—tried to convey this by writing of the "exquisite delight" to be "savored" in the most personal, intimate, "secret" parts of a person while they "chew the bread" of God's word.

Lectio divina invites every one of us into this kind of intimate encounter, to a table spread for us alone but where there is always room for one more guest.

In *lectio divina*, one reads slowly (each session might last thirty to sixty minutes), thoughtfully, and deeply, in four steps, called by their Latin names: *lectio, meditatio, oratio,* and *contemplatio.*

- ✦ *Lectio* is reading, analogous to a bite, for the one who is feasting on God's word.

⊕ *Meditatio* is meditating, considering what the words have to offer; the chewing phase.

⊕ *Oratio* is praying, savoring what you have tasted, speaking to God about it, and listening for what God may have to say in response.

⊕ *Contemplatio* is contemplating, or resting in God's loving presence, akin to digesting nutritious, delicious food lovingly prepared.

How do these four steps work in practice?

First, choose a text. It should be short: a line or two of a psalm, or a verse or (at most) two from a gospel or other favorite book of the Old or New Testament. "The Lord is my shepherd; I shall not be in want" is a good candidate; so is, "Arise, shine, for your light has come, and the glory of the Lord has risen upon you" (Isaiah 60:1); or "Jesus woke up and rebuked the wind, and said to the sea, 'Peace! Be still!' Then the wind ceased, and there was a dead calm" (Mark 4:39). Unlike Ignatian imaginative prayer, in which you place yourself in a larger story, adding details based on what you imagine being able to perceive with your senses, the idea in lectio divina is to focus sharply on a shorter passage of scripture. That piece should be bite-sized, small enough to allow yourself to taste it fully.

Second, read the text slowly, at least twice. Hear each word, and let the whole phrase or verse enter your consciousness. This is the *lectio* phase (although the umbrella term *lectio divina* applies to the whole practice, approaching the text—whether reading it yourself or hearing it read in audiobook form or by a group leader—is step one, *lectio*).

After you have read the text a couple of times, move into the *meditatio* phase. Consider: what word or few words particularly spoke to you or seemed to have special significance? Reflect on them; notice what thoughts and feelings arise in response to them. The word or phrase that strikes you may be deeply familiar or may surprise you; likewise, your response may be one you have had many times or completely new. Simply notice your responses without judging them, and then hold them in mind as you read the text again, slowly (repeating the *meditatio* step).

You may find it helpful to close your eyes during this step and the next (*oratio*) to shut out distractions. If you need a focal point beyond the words of your chosen passage to help you concentrate or to create a sacred space for *lectio divina*, you might place an icon of Jesus or a beloved saint, or a favorite photograph, beside you, or practice in a spot with a pleasant view. When you lift your eyes from the page to meditate, pray, or contemplate, the image or view will be there to help you focus.

As I've noted above, *meditatio* is the step of lectio divina that has most been compared to chewing. Many practitioners of *lectio divina* use the metaphor of rumination to describe this step. If you have been treated for depression or anxiety, the word "rumination" may have negative associations for you: in that context, it refers to obsessively repeating a disturbing or self-harmful thought without reaching a resolution. Rumination, in the context of *lectio divina*, has a different meaning. Here, noting the thoughts and feelings that arise in you in response to the text is akin to a cow chewing her cud to extract the greatest nutritional benefit from the grass that builds up her body and keeps her milk flowing. This rumination is productive, pleasant, and instructive, not obsessive or distressing.

After you have considered your response to the text, meditated on it, chewed it over, move to the *oratio* step—if you have not already, spontaneously done so. As you read the text once more, slowly, notice: what prayer arises from your reflection? It may be a prayer of supplication, adoration, intercession, confession, or any of the other classic types. Noticing this prayer, offering it to God silently or out loud, and listening for any divine response, is the savoring portion of this practice.

We usually think of "savoring" as a pleasant experience, but if the prayer that wells up from you is one of confession, the moment may not seem like something to savor. Consider, though, the opportunity that confession gives you to reflect on a way you have fallen short of God's desire for you, a way you have not loved God, your neighbor, or yourself in the way you truly want to. And consider the truth that God already knows your heart, is always ready to accept your confession and will strengthen you as you seek, once more, to live as a disciple of Jesus. In his description of spiritual consolation, Ignatius of Loyola included not only the movements of the soul that cause one to be "inflamed with love of God" and a sense of "tranquility and peace" in the love of God but also "tears of grief for [the soul's] own sins" that move one closer to God.[6] Whatever type of prayer you offer in this step of *oratio* can draw you closer to God and equip you to participate in revealing God's loving power in the world.

The fourth step of *lectio divina* may or may not occur in any discernible way on any given occasion of prayer. Through reading and prayer, we may arrive at *contemplatio*, resting in God's love. I say "may" because, after reading, listening, and praying, we won't necessarily feel, every time, a heightened awareness of God's enfolding love. While that may be disappointing, it doesn't mean God is not present or that our prayer is not valid, or that *lectio* isn't "working" as it "should." The true measure of whether we are resting in God's love may be found less in a feeling than in our actions: the ways in which our prayer, the time we devote to being consciously in God's company, affects how we live.

Lectio divina, like any prayer practice, will change us over time, not just during periods of active prayer but also through the Holy Spirit's ongoing work within us. We might call this process of scripture changing us the "digestion" phase of *lectio divina*, in which God's Word becomes integrated into us at the most fundamental levels. A sixteenth-century Anglican prayer, still used today, asks God "who caused all holy scriptures to be written for our learning" to help us "so to hear them, read, mark, learn, and inwardly digest them, that we may embrace and ever hold fast the blessed hope of everlasting life" (The Book of Common Prayer, 236). Through the Bible, God invites us to a delicious, nutritious feast that will change who we are and what we do. *Lectio divina* is one way to give our "yes" to that invitation.

Questions to consider and things to try

✠ As you begin to practice *lectio divina*, you might feel overwhelmed by the prospect of choosing a short passage of scripture with which to pray. I suggest choosing a verse from the previous or upcoming Sunday's lectionary passages or working with a guide like Thelma Hall, RC, *Too Deep For Words: Rediscovering Lectio Divina* (Mahwah, NJ: Paulist Press, 1988) or Martin L. Smith, *The Word is Very Near You: A Guide to Praying with Scripture* (Cambridge, MA: Cowley Publications, 1989).[7]

✠ Practice *lectio divina* with some pre-determined frequency for a period of time, say, daily for two weeks or weekly for six weeks. At the end of each session, jot down a few notes about each step of the process. What word, words, or phrase stood out for you? What thoughts, feelings, prayers arose in you? Did anything surprise, comfort, or disturb you? Did you have a sense of God's presence or absence? Remember that God is always with you, whether or not you feel the divine presence. If you grow concerned about any thoughts or feelings that arise from this or any prayer practice, share those concerns with a clergyperson, friend, therapist, or other trusted companion.

✠ Practice *lectio divina* with a friend or small group. The group may choose to briefly share reflections after each step, or not. If participants do share, remember that each person's offerings are personal and valid; participants should not argue with each other about their experiences of the scripture.[8]

✠ Return to *lectio divina* at times when you feel overwhelmed either by the world or the demands of your life or by your regular prayer practices. If, for example, Morning and Evening Prayer seems too wordy or you feel weighed down by trying to "accomplish" too much in prayer, consider taking small bites from the feast of God's word, chewing them over slowly and contemplatively, and accepting whatever gift—including simple rest—the experience may offer.

⊕ You might consider what some call *visio divina:* praying with icons or images. Former Archbishop of Canterbury Rowan Williams offers guidance on praying with icons in two small books: *Ponder These Things: Praying with Icons of the Virgin* (Franklin, WI: Sheed & Ward, 2002), and *The Dwelling of the Light: Praying with Icons of Christ* (Grand Rapids, MI: Wm. B. Eerdmans Publishing Co., 2004).

Endnotes

[1] *The Rule of St. Benedict in English,* trans. and ed. Timothy Fry, osb, (Collegeville, MN: The Liturgical Press, 1982), 48:1.

[2] Ambrose of Milan, "On the Duties of the Clergy," I:32:165, https://www.newadvent.org/fathers/34011.htm, accessed 12 February 2021.

[3] Augustine, *The Confessions,* trans. Maria Boulding, osb, and ed. John E. Rotelle, osa, (Hyde Park, N.Y.: New City Press, 1997), 6:3.

[4] Augustine, *The Confessions*, 137, n.20.

[5] Speaking to the believers at Miletus, in Acts 20:32.

[6] "The Spiritual Exercises" 316, in Ignatius of Loyola and George E. Ganss, sj, *Ignatius of Loyola: Spiritual Exercises and Selected Works* (Mahwah, NJ: Paulist Press, 1991).

[7] You can find the Revised Common Lectionary at http://lectionarypage.net/.

[8] An obvious exception would be if a participant were to understand scripture to justify a sin like murder. Even then, it would be more helpful for their prayer companions to seek to understand how the person arrived at such an interpretation and to find help for them if necessary than to argue.

Praying Through Music

Be thou my vision, O Lord of my heart; naught be all else to me, save that thou art...

Wade in the water; wade in the water, children...

O Holy Night, the stars are brightly shining; it is the night of our dear Savior's birth...

Lift every voice and sing, 'til earth and heaven ring; ring with the harmonies of liberty...

In the late spring of 2020, I surprised myself by bursting into song at random moments. This was not just quietly humming as I loaded the dishwasher or refilled the backyard birdfeeder, as had been my wont before the coronavirus pandemic upended the world that winter. No, I frequently found myself belting out songs, singing at the top of my lungs before I had even realized lyrics had entered my mind.

That's probably because the songs didn't have far to travel. They had been laid deep into my soul over my two decades as a practicing

Christian. The songs I found myself singing were some of my favorites: the ones that made me smile widely, or cry, or smile through tears, in church. Or they had, before churches suddenly shut our buildings, doing our part to slow the deadly virus's spread. A couple of months in, as I grieved the pandemic's toll—as I sat bewildered before governments' inability to contain the pandemic or effectively relieve the suffering it caused, and as news reports and citizen-recorded videos of killings of unarmed Black people proliferated—these songs flowed out of my mouth as fervent prayers. And they continued to do so as the year 2020 departed and I watched and prayed for whatever would follow those challenging times.

Often coming to me out of season, these songs put flesh on my emotions at a time when I had grown weary of groping for words to express my feelings to God. "O, Holy Night," in July was an appeal to God who had been born into the world as a helpless baby, at a time when children were experiencing all the deprivations and dangers of the pandemic. At the same time, the song made me smile as I looked forward to a Christmas Eve when I would gather again with fellow Christians to watch children put on a pageant and to sing favorite carols together. The words from the hymn, "Humbly I adore thee, Verity unseen," affirmed my sense that Jesus Christ was with the world at a time when the pandemic cut me and most Christians I knew off from the eucharist.[1] And voicing hymns that were written to be sung by a congregation expressed both my longing to hear again a congregation's polyvocal (and sometimes, frankly, inharmonious) offering, and my hope that, one day, I would.

That prayers erupted from me in the form of song was a surprise. I love to sing, but it doesn't come easily to me. In fact, I went through several sessions with a hypnotherapist to overcome my phobia of chanting the eucharist. (The hypnosis worked pretty well.) My shyness around singing runs so deep that I wouldn't have expected familiar melodies and lyrics would spring to my aid when my own facility with words failed me.

When we are in despair and at a loss, as I was at times during the pandemic, God continues to reach out to us. God keeps offering us ways to connect to the Divine and to the communion of saints, to lament and to dare to hope that our experience might yet be redeemed and maybe, even, sanctified. The melodies that sustained me in the pandemic have been hallowed by generations of singers— who, I believe, continue to sing God's praises and intercede for God's children on earth. Some of these songs sustained me decades ago when I started attending church after my mother's death and would frequently sit through services doing nothing but cry as the congregation read, prayed, and made music around me. Music touches us at a deep emotional level, where intellectual and physical defenses are stripped away. And once those walls are down, when we are vulnerable, we open to God.

"The one who sings, prays twice." I can't count the number of times I've heard a devout chorister or music director repeat this quote, attributed to Saint Augustine of Hippo, or how often I've seen it, framed, hanging on choir-room walls.

What Augustine actually wrote is even more beautiful (but, sadly, doesn't fit as well into an eight-by-ten frame). "For the one who sings praise, does not only praise, but also praises joyfully; the one who sings praise, not only sings, but also loves Him to whom he is singing. In praise [of God], there is a confession, a public proclamation; in the song of the lover, love."[2]

Augustine may have been getting at the emotional and physical energy we put into singing. Our whole body gets involved: muscles, lungs, brain, heart, limbs. Our toes and fingers tap, our facial expressions change, we may dance. We can feel the joy or longing at the heart of the composition seeping or exploding into us. We experience the music's vibration from inside and, if we're singing along with others or to instruments, from outside ourselves too. If ever you're tempted to see prayer as something your "mind" or "soul" does separately from your body, then singing praises or laments to

God, feeling the vibrations in your chest as you draw in air and push out sound, shows how mistaken that view is.

Instrumental music can be just as much a prayer as singing. The Bible's final psalm calls God's people to praise the Lord with every instrument at their disposal. Here it is in its entirety:

> Hallelujah!
> Praise God in his holy temple;
> praise him in the firmament of his power.
> Praise him for his mighty acts;
> praise him for his excellent greatness.
> Praise him with the blast of the ram's-horn;
> praise him with lyre and harp.
> Praise him with timbrel and dance;
> praise him with strings and pipe.
> Praise him with resounding cymbals;
> praise him with loud-clanging cymbals.
> Let everything that has breath
> praise the Lord.
> Hallelujah!

Psalm 150 sums up a book that is full of laments, complaints, and howls for retribution as well as praises and thanksgivings. The final song is a call to praise because even in those times when we fall into a pit of despair, God who inspired the psalms still seeks us out and will listen to whatever is on our minds. This truth about God is, itself, worthy of praise.

Michael Curry, presiding bishop of the Episcopal Church, has written about this kind of praise song; songs like "There is a balm in Gilead," "His eye is on the sparrow," "Go down, Moses." All four of his grandparents were themselves the grandchildren of formerly enslaved people, and from those grandparents, Curry gained an understanding of how his ancestors had prayed their way through trials and thanksgivings, often in song. "Their songs and sayings reflected a deep faith and profound wisdom that taught them how to shout 'glory' while cooking in 'sorrow's kitchen,'" he writes. "In this, there was a hidden treasure that saw many of them through, and that is now a spiritual inheritance for those of us who have come after them. That treasure was a sung faith expressing a way of being in relationship with the living God of Jesus that was real, energizing, sustaining, loving, liberating, and life-giving."[3] Bishop Curry's family knew that their oppressors neither understood nor defined them and that white people's attempts to constrain their freedom—their very being—violated God's will. They proclaimed that truth, they contested white Christians' blasphemy, and they praised God and prayed for deliverance in song.[4]

It may be appropriate that I turned, unwittingly, toward song in what felt in many ways like a desert season. I usually rely on music to carry me through Lent. It's a season when Christians remember Jesus's trials in the desert and anticipate his Passion by examinations of conscience, persisting more deeply in prayer, and fasting from certain types of food or other pleasures. And it's a season that has always been hard for me, by a fluke of the calendar: Lent often falls in February, and February is the month when my mother attempted suicide more than once and then, one year, completed the act.[5] The aftereffects of years of witnessing her pain and enduring the turbulence and abuse that came with it, and then living with her death drive me into my own personal wilderness annually.

In that desert, my own words often fail me, and others feel inadequate, but instrumental music seeps into my wounds and soothes them. It serves as the healing balm that Bishop Curry's ancestors affirmed God would, indeed, provide for devastated people. Those ancestors' songs answered the question the prophet Jeremiah posed millennia ago, as he witnessed the Babylonian conquest of his nation: "Is there no balm in Gilead? Is there no physician there? Why then has the health of my poor people not been restored?"[6] There are moments, whether in a personal tragedy or in a catastrophe on the scale of a pandemic, when one can only exclaim with Jeremiah, "O that my head were a spring of water, and my eyes a fountain of tears, so that I might weep day and night for the slain of my poor people!"[7] At various times in my life, I have cried hard enough to have left myself with a raging thirst; I have blubbered through necessary daily tasks like brushing my teeth, frothing up a salty, foamy mess; and I have sat in an arid, stony grief beyond tears.

A composition that stirs and soothes me in all those states, and to which I return every Lent, is "A Love Supreme," virtuoso jazz performer John Coltrane's exploration of healing and spiritual rebirth. Recorded in 1964, the album was inspired by Coltrane's experience of God's presence during his withdrawal from heroin several years earlier. During that hellish yet revelatory experience, as Coltrane wrote in the album's original liner notes, "I humbly asked to be given the means and privilege to make others happy through music." After recording what turned out to be a more influential work than he could have imagined, Coltrane was able to add, "I feel this has been granted through His grace" in the album he presented as "a humble offering to Him."[8] Through the four movements of the piece—"Acknowledgement," "Resolution," "Pursuance," and "Psalm"—Coltrane and his fellow musicians put musical flesh on the poem he wrote and included in the album:

> *The fact that we exist is acknowledgment of Thee O Lord.*
> *Thank you God.*
> *God will wash away all our tears...*
> *He always has...*
> *He always will.*
> *Seek Him every day. In all ways seek God every day.*[9]

In Lent, and at other trying times, listening to heartfelt instrumental music gives me joy. It's my way of seeking God; of reminding myself that God is always seeking me out, in part through messengers like John Coltrane. As a musician raised in the church, Coltrane likely knew that the Bible says a young David, future king of Israel, was called in to play his harp for Saul at moments when the king was in spiritual torment: "And whenever the evil spirit from God came upon Saul, David took the lyre and played it with his hand, and Saul would be relieved and feel better, and the evil spirit would depart from him." Decades after Coltrane's death, his music still offers this gift of healing.

Making music with other people can be a form of prayer, just as much as listening contemplatively to music others have created. Having sung in a couple of choirs, I have been moved by the interplay and blend of voices and by the staggering, soaring beauty of soloists who reach heights and depths I will never attain. I have felt the solidarity of mixing my breath with a choral section as, together, we put flesh on the composer's creation. As a priest and a worshiper of the Triune God, I have closed my eyes and sighed in appreciation of an offertory that expressed more than I could ever preach about why we had gathered that day, and I have joined my voice with the rest of the congregation to sing praises, laments, and petitions. Over and over, as siblings in Christ and I emulated millennia of our ancestors in faith by singing together, I have felt that we were responding to the invitation of God who delights in our efforts in something the same way, maybe, as parents delight in a baby's babbles and in a budding instrumentalist's uncertain but dogged practice.

When we address God in music and song, we accept the psalmist's ancient invitation, "Serve the Lord with gladness and come before his presence with a song," and we follow in the path of the early church as attested in the Letter to the Ephesians, whose members were exhorted to "be filled with the Spirit, as you sing psalms and hymns and spiritual songs among yourselves, singing and making melody to the Lord in your hearts."[10]

These psalms, hymns, and songs set down deep roots. We remember words set to music more easily, probably because the rhythm, rhyme, and (sometimes) alliteration of lyrics serve to cement them in our memories. This is why we teach children the alphabet through a song. Having studied both biblical Hebrew and Greek as an adult, I can attest to the mnemonic function of melody: I learned a Hebrew alphabet song, but not a Greek one, and only the former has stuck with me. And the more often one sings or hears a song, and the deeper its emotional resonance, the more likely one is to remember it, even after suffering dementia or other memory loss.

That's why beloved hymns flowed through my lips as pandemic prayers; that's why the repeated "Alleluias" of Easter hymns make me beam with joy every single year; that's why people with dementia can often still recite the Lord's Prayer, warble a long-favored hymn, and sing along with "Happy Birthday." And that's why, when I reach the end of my earthly life, I hope I may leave this world surrounded by friends who will pray and sing with me—or who will simply sing because, with the right intention, prayer and song are one and the same.

Questions to consider and things to try

✛ Do you have a favorite hymn or another piece of music that you think perfectly expresses something of who God is or who you are in relation to God? Devote a few quiet minutes to listening to it and thanking God for it. Perhaps invite a friend to join you, each of you choosing a piece to share with the other.

✛ Set aside some time to listen to a musical piece that is new to you and that others have found meaningful. You might consider Taizé chants, Bach's St. John Passion or Mass in B Minor, Sweet Honey in the Rock, Kendrick Lamar's "DAMN," or Leonard Cohen's "You Want It Darker," or ask a friend for a suggestion. In what ways does the music deepen your appreciation of the world's beauty? In what ways does it open your eyes to or affirm your understanding of suffering? Offer those insights to God.

✛ Develop a playlist for a liturgical season that is either particularly challenging for you (as Lent is for me) or particularly joyful. What music comforts you when you need it or explores pain and redemption in helpful ways as "A Love Supreme" does for me? What music expresses joy and praises God, implicitly or explicitly? Put together some selections and listen to them in God's company.

✛ Consider: what hymns would you like sung at your funeral? If you reach conclusions, write them down and leave them with your will. You might share your selections with a close family member or friend or your clergyperson.

✛ Sing! By yourself, with a friend or group of friends, as you are able. Select a favorite hymn, a Taizé chant, a song that you remember a grandparent or another nurturing figure in your life enjoying. Thank God for the music, the relationships it reminds you of—and perhaps its power to help heal wounds from those relationships—and for your ability, whatever that might be, to make and/or appreciate a joyful noise to the Lord.

Endnotes

[1] "Humbly I adore thee," *The Hymnal 1982* (New York: Church Publishing Inc., 1985), #314.

[2] From Augustine's commentary on the 72nd Psalm. Latin text at http://www.augustinus.it/latino/esposizioni_salmi/index2.htm, accessed 20 December 2020; cited in Ruth A. Meyers, *Missional Worship, Worshipful Mission: Gathering as God's People, Going Out in God's Name* (Grand Rapids, MI: Eerdmans, 2014), 225. By "confession," Augustine means an acknowledgment or proclamation of faith.

[3] Michael B. Curry, *Songs My Grandma Sang* (New York: Morehouse Publishing, 2015), 2.

[4] To journey more deeply into African American spirituals, you might read and pray with Mark Bozzuti-Jones, *Face to the Rising Sun* (Cincinnati: Forward Movement, 2021), or devotionals by Luke Powery: *Rise Up, Shepherd! Advent Reflections on the Spirituals* (Louisville: Westminster John Knox, 2017) and *Were You There? Lenten Reflections on the Spirituals* (Louisville: Westminster John Knox, 2018).

[5] I have written about my experience of Lent at https://faithandleadership.com/rhonda-mawhood-lee-not-giving-lent.

[6] Jeremiah 8:22.

[7] Jeremiah 9:1.

[8] John Coltrane. Liner notes for *A Love Supreme*. Impulse! Records, 1965.

[9] Ellipses in the original.

[10] Psalm 100:1; Ephesians 5:18-19.

Praying Through Movement

For three or four years in my twenties, I practiced martial arts, devoting five hours a week to Shorin-ryu karate, a traditional Okinawan style, and Arnis, the Filipino weapons-based art. The dojo (or studio) where I practiced was run for women by women who made sure practical self-defense and conflict de-escalation were also regular parts of our training. Four days a week, I moved in tandem with dozens of other women, punching and kicking our way up and down the dojo. I learned progressively more challenging kicks, punches, and blocks and incorporated them into forms, the highly choreographed sparring matches against a real or imaginary opponent that are the foundation of any martial art. My body became more toned, and my spirit more confident. I learned to take up space, to claim my own strength, and to use an opponent's energy against them. I realized that the same attribute—say, my long arms and legs—could be an advantage, hitting an opponent far from me, or a disadvantage, making it hard to reach a smaller opponent who got in close to my body.

And I learned lessons that have stayed with me in the decades since I stopped practicing: that we all have aggressive impulses and need to develop positive ways to channel them. That my body was stronger than I'd ever imagined, and that bodies of all sizes, shapes, and abilities have their own strengths and beauties. That conflict is not something to fear and engaging in it can be healthy. That pushing too hard can be counter-productive.

I left the dojo after a few years because I started attending, and then got deeply involved in, church, and I didn't have time and energy to devote to both communities of practice. But lessons from years of grueling and playful hours stayed with me as I learned how to serve as a lay minister and then discerned and followed a call to ordination. My most important insights were about practice: things I learned through movement became most deeply a part of me; I needed a community of practice to help me learn, and to keep me going through the moments when I wanted to give up; and whatever habits I repeated over and over would become a part of me, for better or worse.

Everything martial arts taught me remains true and transferable to my life as a Christian. What I lost on joining the church was a regular physical spiritual practice. I jogged and did light strength training, and I walked with friends, but I didn't have a practice that emphasized the unity of body, mind, and spirit the way my work in the dojo had. Prayer usually involved a lot of words—and sitting (mostly) still.

But a number of prayer practices do involve movement. If prayer is time devoted to being consciously in the presence of God, speaking, listening, or in companionable silence, there's no requirement that the person praying sit, kneel, or otherwise keep still during that time. For many people, sitting still is a physical or mental challenge. For others, like parents of small children, it might be hard to sit still, at home, without being interrupted. For some of us, movement might awaken a sense of God's presence in a way that sitting still cannot. And for many of us, in moments when words fail us, when we can't find the words to express our needs and hopes, when words feel inadequate or sound false, it's reassuring to know God doesn't need them to enjoy our company.

The practices I discuss in this chapter are not an exhaustive list of ways to pray through movement. They simply offer a brief survey of a few ways to consciously integrate body, mind, and spirit in our relationship with God: praying the labyrinth, running (or jogging, walking, or swimming), yoga, "praying in color,"[1] and what I call "praying through chores." In your explorations, you may discover other ways or you may already have a movement practice you enjoy. If that's the case, I hope these reflections lead you to deeper insights into the gifts your practice offers.

I first encountered the word "labyrinth" as a child in the ancient Greek legend of the Minotaur. There, it referred to the elaborate maze the artist Daedalus built for King Minos of Crete. The labyrinth's many twists, turns, and blind alleys served not only to keep the Minotaur imprisoned but also to trap the young men and women who were, periodically, fed alive to the monstrous man-bull.

Not a promising association for a practice that's supposed to bring human beings closer to God.

But prayer labyrinths are different. This form of walking meditation, found in many cultures, predates Christianity and was adopted by the Church within its first few centuries. The best-known Christian labyrinth was built at Chartres Cathedral in the eleventh century; countless others have been modeled on it. Unlike Daedalus's elaborate prison, the Christian labyrinth is an unbroken circular path leading to a central point and back out again. There's one path in and one path out, no blind alleys, no cunning builder to outwit, and no lurking monster—except perhaps the fears we bring to the practice. If you set out on a Christian labyrinth and keep going, you *will* reach your destination. And then you can return safely to your starting point, perhaps a little bit changed by the journey. The labyrinth walk is a mini-pilgrimage, a metaphor for the Christian life: our gracious God is always ready to receive us, our wise God will guide us, our loving God will not let us fall off the path toward the Divine.

You've probably seen a labyrinth somewhere. Churches build them outside, of bricks, stone, colored glass, even low hedges; sometimes they lay indoor labyrinths of tile; often, they purchase or create portable labyrinths painted on canvas that can be laid down for a retreat day or Lenten practice. You may also have seen a finger labyrinth: a flat disc embracing the labyrinth's circular shape, to be traced contemplatively when walking a labyrinth (or rolling in a wheelchair) isn't possible.

When you're ready to pray the labyrinth, the main thing is, you can't hurry. Take a deep breath or three. Quiet your mind as much as possible. In the midst of whatever you are thinking and feeling, take a moment to address God. What you say could be as simple as, "I'm here," "Hello," "I need you," or "I'm happy to be with you." If you have something specific on your mind—a worry, a sin to confess, a pattern of behavior or events you're wondering about—state it briefly, either silently or out loud. You don't need to have anything specific on your mind; the desire to pass some time consciously in God's company is the only reason you need to be there.

Move slowly toward the center, feeling the connection between your feet and the path, or your finger and the disc, or your arms and your wheelchair armrests, or your eyes and the path ahead, as best fits your mobility. As you move deliberately, focus on being present with God who is eager for your company. If you have brought a problem with you, focus less on the problem itself than on offering it to God; less, "Why did I do that thing?" and more, "Lord, I did this thing, and I am truly sorry; in your compassion, forgive me and guide me." The journey into the center of the labyrinth is a time to release your concerns into God's care. Those concerns won't necessarily be gone forever, but by releasing them, you are entrusting them to God, reminding yourself that God wants to help you, and you are praying for a resolution in line with God's purposes.

When you reach the center, take time consciously to receive whatever gifts this prayer time may have given you. You may have experienced a sense of peace and well-being or an insight about a path to take next, and you may feel moved to give thanks. You may have experienced nothing extraordinary or even disappointment that nothing special happened during your prayer. Whatever feelings you may have, it is a safe and holy thing to acknowledge them in God's presence.

As you return from the center to the beginning of the labyrinth, still moving slowly, remain as open-hearted as you can. Notice your breath; notice your feelings; remember that God is with you. As you conclude your labyrinth prayer, give thanks, again, for any gifts you received and for the grace to respond to God's invitation to pass some time together.

For some people, running, jogging, walking, swimming, or other whole-body athletic activities are a devotional practice. The Scottish runner Eric Liddell felt this way. He took a gold and a bronze at the 1924 Olympics, passing up a chance at two more medals because he wouldn't compete on Sunday. The devout joy and union with the Divine that Liddell felt in running was memorialized in the film "Chariots of Fire," in which his character explains why he's so devoted to training: "I believe God made me for a purpose, but he also made me fast. And when I run I feel His pleasure." After the Olympics, Liddell became a Presbyterian missionary teacher in China; he died in an internment camp during the Japanese occupation of the Second World War. I wonder if, toward the end, he may have remembered the line from the Second Letter to Timothy that honors athletic metaphors for the Christian life: "I have fought the good fight, I have finished the race, I have kept the faith."[2]

American writer Jamie Quatro expresses the prayerful nature of running in her own way. For her, deep prayer comes in what she calls a third "layer" of consciousness on a long run. This state succeeds the initial pleasure of the endorphin rush and then the "delusions of grandeur" these natural chemicals induce, in which Quatro imagines herself "standing in front of applauding audiences." The third layer is "a state of prayerlike consciousness," when her attention moves outward to the world through which her feet are pounding, her senses pick up details she might normally miss, and she feels connected to the universal in a way beyond her daily experience. "It's a paradox," she writes. "Only when I'm fully present in my body do I begin to experience the absence of myself." Running takes Quatro out of her own way, so that she can experience God's closeness.[3]

Relatively few people are devoted long-distance runners; even fewer compete in the Olympics. But even a quiet stroll, or a 5K or 3K run, or a 1000-meter swim can be a prayer, when it's entered into with that intention. Put your phone and earbuds away, and settle into the movement you've chosen. If quieting your thoughts is a challenge, focus on your breathing and the movement of your limbs (or the forward roll of your mobility aid). Give thanks for your ability to move in whatever ways you can and for your breath and heartbeat. As you sink deeper into the rhythm of your movement, notice what catches your attention—birdsong? Children playing? A person talking alone?—and give thanks or offer an intercessory prayer for them as the Spirit moves you. Approach your movement prayer as companionable time with a beloved friend, who delights in you and wants only the best for you and give thanks for whatever fruit this time bears.

My friend Kelly's experience doing yoga is reminiscent of Eric Liddell's insights about running. She remembers feeling "unbridled joy" doing a headstand for the first time, and also awe. "I just glowed when it was done," thinking, "My God, my body can do that! What a marvelous thing God has made! My body can do all kinds of things I didn't know it could do." Practicing yoga has helped Kelly, as she says, "view my body as I think God views my body." In the studio, she's not thinking about how she would like to lose a few pounds or look a certain way in a bathing suit; she's not wishing her body could still do everything it could when she was young. "The practice of yoga," she has learned, "is so much about being in your body and being grateful for it, and honoring it." Or, as Christian yoga practitioners and authors Amy Dolan and Hillary Raining put it, "Yoga teaches us to love ourselves as God's creation."[4] And that's true whether, like Kelly, we can do a headstand, or whether our movements are more limited. Yoga poses can be endlessly adapted to each person's abilities.

Honoring our bodies in all their diversity is something the church could do better. Tradition proclaims that our bodies are God's good creation and that we will be raised, body and soul, at the end of days. Human beings are bodies and souls, both, together; we could be described as "ensouled" bodies and "enfleshed" souls. But Christianity has often treated the two as separable, denigrating the body while elevating the soul. And this separation has gone hand-in-hand with abuses of power. The church has harmed people regarded as more subject to the body's whims, like women, children, and people with disabilities, and it has protected people—mostly men—who have hurt others in the name of God.

A devout Episcopalian, Kelly has found in the yoga studio a unity of body and soul and an intimacy among practitioners that is often missing in Christian communities. This has especially been true as she has lived through painful moments. With permission, yoga instructors touch their students' bodies in class to adjust a pose or urge a student to relax a tight muscle. As a result, Kelly says, "They come close to your pain and to your tender spots. Sometimes, we Christians are tentative about getting close to each other's tender spots." Given the history of abuse in the Church, there are good reasons for Christians to be cautious about touching each other. But we could do more to foster intimacy in our communities, to make it easier to open up about our tender spots, and to honor each other's bruises, aches, and scars. If we cultivated that kind of intimacy, we would experience closer communion with God and each other, which is the purpose of prayer.

Because yoga comes from the Hindu tradition, not all Christians feel comfortable practicing it. They may not want to appear to be worshiping in a different tradition, or they may have concerns about appropriating a practice from a culture that was colonized by professed Christians. And while many Hindus don't mind Christians borrowing this practice, many others wish we wouldn't. One Methodist layperson I know prays for God's guidance before doing yoga so that if her practice should be leading her away from Jesus she would become aware of that and stop. Another acquaintance, a Presbyterian deacon, appreciates the benefits yoga gives her without thinking of the practice, itself, as prayer. "When I first started practicing," she says, "I did have concerns. It didn't feel right to fold my hands in prayer, and bow to someone else [rather than the Triune God]." Now, however, she finds beauty in "the idea of *Namaste*," honoring another person "from my heart to your heart." Resting firmly on the conviction that there is only one God and giving thanks for the balance, self-awareness, and physical and mental strength yoga gives her, my deacon acquaintance integrates these gifts into her prayer life. If you're considering yoga as a prayer practice, I suggest exploring the questions of compatibility with Christianity and cultural appropriation as part of your discernment.[5]

As praying with finger labyrinths has shown us, movement prayers don't have to involve the whole body. Moving one's fingers can be enough to change one's perspective, engage a different part of one's brain, and offer a new experience of prayer. That's the insight behind "praying in color," Sybil MacBeth's practice of prayerful doodling. When writer and Christian spirituality professor Lauren Winner asked a class at the North Carolina women's prison what effect they thought "praying in color" over several years would have on their relationship with God, one participant answered, "Fun. I think my relationship with God would be fun." As Winner elaborates, "It would be characterized by play, by pleasure, by enjoyment."[6]

That's not to say that MacBeth advocates doodling only happy prayers. The various chapters of her book cover the gamut: intercession, confession, adoration, praying for enemies, 12-step prayers, and more. What her method has given her "is a renewed sense of *delight* in my prayer time," meaning "expectant enthusiasm and energy." All of us can use that kind of expectancy, an infusion of energy, from time to time, especially when we feel as if our words have gone stale or abandoned us completely. And if, like MacBeth, we "need a way to pray that suits my short attention span, my restless body, and my inclination to live in my head," we might try her method.[7]

No artistic skill is required for this practice; all you need are paper, a few coloring tools, and an openness to experiment. Writing a name of God ("Father" and "Jesus" are classics, but MacBeth suggests others, too, like "One," "Mystery," or "Redeemer") and the names of those for whom we are interceding, the sins we are confessing, or the matter about which we are discerning, and then connecting these words through simple lines, shapes, and squiggles, all in color: all of this is time devoted to God's company. All of it is prayer.

When I "pray in color," I notice a few things. My breathing slows. From time to time, I nod or smile, in unbidden acknowledgement of the calm that has taken me over. I move beyond performance anxiety, the search for the "perfect" words to address God, into a state of anticipation, waiting to see which colors my heart will choose and where my fingers will lead. Sometimes the practice gives me a new insight; sometimes not. Sometimes I admire what I have drawn; sometimes not. Always, I gain a sense of having passed time in companionable silence with someone dear to me.

What about those times, or those seasons of life, when one can't seem to set aside time to pray? Maybe there are children underfoot; maybe work seems to consume every hour of the day. Chances are, this situation won't last forever. While it does, one can still enter consciously into the presence of God, by doing the things one has to do anyway, in a prayerful spirit. One can pray through chores.

That's the insight offered by Brother Lawrence, a seventeenth-century French Carmelite whose letters and conversations were collected into a volume that has become a classic of Christian spirituality, *The Practice of the Presence of God*.[8] A veteran of the Thirty Years' War, Lawrence joined his community as a lay brother, not ordained and devoted primarily to manual labor. Lawrence wrote that "We may make an oratory of our heart wherein to retire from time to time to converse with [God] in meekness, humility, and love," even in the midst of daily chores.[9] By recalling that one is always in the presence of God, and by bringing one's mind back to God when it wanders, any ordinary, wholesome task can be a prayer.[10] I know a mother who, inspired by Brother Lawrence, prayed as she folded mountains of her toddlers' laundry—one of the few moments she had to herself in the long days of those short years. The focus of her prayers radiated outward and then back in as she folded: for her children; for other people's children, especially those in distress or danger; for various needs in her community, or situations she had heard about on the news; and for herself. *Fold, pray, smooth, pray, stack, pray…*her laundry room, and her heart, became an oratory of the kind Brother Lawrence spoke.

Episcopal priest Barbara Brown Taylor writes of "the grace of physical labor" that she has found on her farm, "[b]ending and rising to hang laundry on the line, kneeling to scrub the yellow pollen off the back porch, hauling bales of fragrant hay up to the loft, raking the chicken pens and gathering the eggs…"[11] This work, Taylor has found, "gives me life," and yet she recognizes that her freedom to do it, or not, sets her apart from those who have no choice but to earn their living through the physical labor that others denigrate. I never asked my mother or her mother whether they found grace in their household tasks. I suspect they didn't. They were too busy juggling unpaid work inside the home with paid work outside and, in my grandmother's case, stretching all available resources to just barely cover her family's needs. But for many people who have been pushed into domestic work or other physical labor, paid, unpaid, or enslaved, a sense of God's presence may well remind them that they have dignity and worth far beyond what their exploiters would ever acknowledge.

The next time you have laundry to fold, or dishes to wash, or a lawn to mow, consider offering that chore to God as a time for the two of you to catch up. If you live with other people, ask not to be interrupted, if possible. Take a deep breath or two and acknowledge that you're in God's presence, and then start your task. Move deliberately, without rushing; feel your movements, rather than doing them automatically. See what prayers bubble up in you: for your household? For neighbors who don't have clean water, or adequate clothing? For workers whose dignity and skill goes unacknowledged? For yourself, that unmet needs would be fulfilled? Any and all of these, and more, are acceptable to lift to the One who loves and values you and your work.

Questions to consider and things to try

✛ Had you used one of the practices in this chapter before reading it? Had you thought of the practice (e.g. doodling) as a prayer before reading the chapter? Did reading the chapter give you any new perspective on that particular form of movement?

✛ Do you have a different physical practice (such as dance, knitting, baking) that you either saw as prayerful, meditative, or contemplative before reading this chapter, or alternatively, had never thought of in that way? How might reading and reflecting on this chapter affect your practice?

✛ Pick one of the practices discussed in this chapter and engage in it for a period of time (maybe once a week for a month). Invite a friend to do the same. Whether you both pick the same practice or not, check in with each other periodically to share your experiences.

✛ Does engaging in any of these practices change the way you see your body, or understand the connections among your body, your soul, and God?

Endnotes

[1] "Praying in color" is a registered trademark owned by Sybil MacBeth, author of *Praying in Color: Drawing a New Path to God* (Brewster, MA: Paraclete Press, 2019).

[2] 2 Timothy 4:7.

[3] Jamie Quatro, "Running As Prayer," https://www.nytimes.com/roomfordebate/2013/06/24/addicted-to-endorphins/running-as-prayer-16, accessed 26 December 2020.

[4] Amy Nobles Dolan and Hillary D. Raining, *Faith with a Twist: A 30-Day Journey into Christian Yoga* (Cincinnati: Forward Movement, 2018; Kindle version), Introduction.

[5] For help in avoiding cultural appropriation through yoga practice, you might consult the work of Susanna Barkataki, such as her book, *Embrace Yoga's Roots: Courageous Ways to Deepen Your Yoga Practice* (Orlando: Ignite Yoga and Wellness Institute, 2020).

[6] Lauren F. Winner, "Foreword," in MacBeth, *Praying in Color*, 13.

[7] You can find an introduction to MacBeth's method at https://prayingincolor.com/.

[8] Available online at https://www.google.com/books/edition/The_Practice_of_the_Presence_of_God/s1I4AQAAMAAJ?hl=en&gbpv=0.

[9] Brother Lawrence, *Practice of the Presence of God*, 49.

[10] I add the qualifier "wholesome" because to state the obvious, sinful acts would not be prayerful, although the realization that one is always in God's presence might be a spur to confess and change.

[11] Barbara Brown Taylor, *An Altar in the World: A Geography of Faith* (New York, HarperOne, 2010), 146.

Silent Prayers

When I meet with people for prayer or counseling, I usually suggest starting our session with silence. Fairly often, the people I meet with are unaccustomed to silence and unsure of how long to wait before speaking, whether to broach whatever's on their mind or to voice their own prayers. In response, I suggest taking three long, deep breaths. This minute or so of silence is a time to allow both parties to catch our breath, literally and figuratively; to remember that we are entering consciously into God's presence; and to set aside, for the length of our time together, whatever might hinder our capacity to listen for the divine voice. The silence acts as a tiny counterweight to our tendency, in this capitalist, achievement-driven culture, to rush from one thing into another without pausing to simply be.

Opening with silence helps everyone present remember that beyond all our words lies a deep silence in which God is waiting and listening to us and for us. Through our own silence, we remind ourselves to wait upon, and listen for, God too.

Sometimes, my companion and I allow the silence to lengthen. As we settle into the wordlessness, as we surrender to the moment, we begin to feel ourselves enfolded into the divine Presence. A brow may furrow, a pair of hands clasp tightly together in focus or fall open in receptiveness, the rhythm of our breath deepen and slow. For a moment or several minutes, we experience what members of the Society of Friends (commonly known as Quakers) call a "gathered" or "covered" meeting. In such a meeting, Quaker mystic Thomas Kelly wrote, "A blanket of divine covering comes over the room, and a quickening Presence pervades us, breaking down some part of the special privacy and isolation of our individual lives and bonding our spirits." In that moment, we realize that "we stand together on holy ground."[1]

In silence, we may become aware of our souls' cries of longing, grumbles of dissatisfaction, whimpers of fear, sighs of pleasure. In silence, we may hear God's response.

Maybe that's why silence can frighten us.

The Bible is filled with testimonies to the prayerful value of silence. The persecuted singer of Psalm 62 defiantly proclaims, "For God alone my soul in silence waits; from him comes my salvation," while in Psalm 46, the divine voice commands the peoples whose anxiety and busyness lead, eventually, to war, "Be still, then, and know that I am God." The composer of Psalm 131 reminds themself, and their community, how self-nurturing it can be simply to rest in God's presence: "I still my soul and make it quiet, like a child upon its mother's breast; my soul is quieted within me."

More than simply advising the faithful to keep silence, scripture assures us that God is present in silence. Even though God speaks to us in words, even though Christians affirm that God is the creative, living, loving Word that called the world into being and still sustains it, God also accompanies us in a silence beyond words.

The phrase most commonly associated with God and silence comes from a story in the First Book of Kings. The prophet Elijah and the foreign Queen Jezebel (consort to Israel's King Ahab) are in conflict over her devotion to foreign gods, her desire to wipe out worship of the God of Israel, and her ruthless abuses of power. In the nineteenth chapter of First Kings, the conflict comes to a head. Elijah manages to kill all Jezebel's prophets, an enraged queen sends her men to hunt down the assailant, and a terrified Elijah flees into hiding. At the precise moment when Elijah has given up all hope of surviving and has even lost his desire to live, God promises to draw near to him. God sends first a great wind, then an earthquake, and then a fire, but the narrator says, "the Lord was not in" any of these. And then, after the fire, comes "a sound of sheer silence." In this silence, Elijah and God find each other; this silence opens the way for a heart-to-heart conversation.[2]

What the New Revised Standard Version of the Bible translates as "a sound of sheer silence" can also be rendered "a still small voice" or "a soft murmuring sound." The point is: even in the midst of tumult, we can find God—God can reach us—in quiet.

As an Episcopal priest, if I want to seek God in silence, I must carve out the time. Beautiful though our Anglican liturgy is, it can leave very little room for quiet. The opportunities, though, are there to be taken: space for the congregation's intercessions and thanksgivings during the prayers of the people; enough time between the call to confession and when the prayer begins for individuals to recall our sinfulness and God's love; an appreciative pause after a particularly beautiful choral piece; a long, holy moment after breaking the consecrated host. The Daily Office prayers are just as wordy as the eucharist, but silence can intentionally be left open to let a reading sink in or to savor a psalm or collect. Leaving time open can lead to discomfort, especially when we're not used to it: throats clearing, eyes opening and looking around, worshipers wondering if the leader has lost their place or if someone has forgotten to stand up and take their part. But it usually doesn't take long for us to get used to a little more silence, to come to expect it, and to settle into it.

Words and silence can complement each other well in worship and prayer. The words of our liturgies are edifying. Drawn mostly from scripture, they build up our familiarity with the stories of our faith, and they cultivate our capacity to place ourselves in those stories and draw hope, conviction, and strength from them. When we listen, truly listen, to the words our ancestors in faith preserved as sacred, we can hear the message they hold for us in our own moment.

And yet, silence has its place in every relationship. Imagine devoting some time to the kind of silent companionship with Jesus that you might enjoy on a walk with a friend or sitting by a stream with a beloved, so quiet that you can hear the leaves rustling, appreciate the complex trills of a bird's song, and maybe even—if you close your eyes and focus—follow the rhythm of the other's breath or heartbeat. These moments are just as vital to the development of a relationship as the mutual self-revelation that comes from sharing our stories, the supportive words we offer in hard times, and the joyful cheers we offer at each other's victories. If silence is an important part of friendship and family life, it might also benefit your relationship with Jesus.

You will notice as you read below about two "silent" practices—centering prayer and the Jesus prayer—that they do use some words. These words serve to ground us, giving us something, metaphorically, to hold onto as we settle into the silence where we will wait for God and where we trust that, somehow, God is already present. Eventually, as you gain practice in these forms of prayer, or as time passes in any one prayer session, the words may drift away, and you may fall truly silent, aware simply of your breath or of a feeling of peace or joy arising from this encounter with God. These experiences are traditionally called "contemplation": resting in God's presence.[3] Using one of the practices I outline here may lead you to such an experience of contemplation. I say "may" rather than "will" because a deep sense of resting in God's presence may or may not arise from prayer. If not, it doesn't mean God is less present with you or loves you less or that you are less faithful than another person or your prayer less effective. The important things to remember are that when you reach out to God, God has already reached out to you; that God always desires your company; and that God will use your prayer for your good and that of your neighbors.

Centering prayer is a practice popularized by Thomas Keating, a twentieth-century Cistercian monk who sought to revive centuries-old Christian contemplative practices.[4] Keating broke centering prayer into four steps.

- ✤ Choose a word to help you focus. Since your intention is to pass time consciously in the presence of God, the word should be something that expresses God to you, like "Jesus," "Love," "Shepherd," "Liberator," "Spirit," "Father," or "Mother."

- ✤ Sit comfortably, shut out distractions, and close your eyes or let your unfocused gaze fall to the floor. Breathe slowly and evenly as you are able (but without fixating on your breath or critiquing your breathing) and offer your focus word as the beginning of your prayer time.

- ✤ As you follow your breath flowing in and out of your lungs and your belly, sink into the silence. When you become aware of thoughts intruding ("What am I going to make for dinner?" "I forgot to put out the recycling"), return gently to your focus word and once again, follow your breath.

- ✤ At the end of your prayer time, stay silent with your eyes closed for a minute or two. Thank God for your time together.

When you start practicing centering prayer, consider setting an alarm for five or ten minutes. (When you're new to silent prayer, ten minutes seems like a very long time.) Knowing that the alarm will go off at the end of your designated prayer time will keep you from being distracted and peeking at the clock. If you desire to keep praying after the alarm sounds, turn it off and keep going. Eventually, your prayer time may stretch to thirty minutes or an hour, but the important thing is to be as present as you can be in this time, however short or long it may be.

Although this is a form of silent prayer, if you feel moved to offer words during this practice, feel free to do so. Centering prayer is not meant to muzzle you. Tell God what you have to say, and then return to following your breath and listening.

Don't despair when you become distracted. It happens to everyone. No less a formidable pray-er than Teresa of Ávila called distractions "unavoidable" and "an incurable disease" that Christians simply need to live with and not spend too much energy worrying about. Likewise, don't berate yourself if you become sleepy. Deep breathing can have that effect on any of us, especially if the practice is new (and maybe this reaction is an invitation to seek out more rest, as you are able). When you are tempted to critique what you see as your failures in this or any new practice of prayer, think of how you would respond to an infant learning to feed itself and covering its face with purée or staggering and falling while learning to walk. You might laugh, and you would certainly stand ready to help, comfort, and clean the child as needed. You wouldn't criticize the child or give up on this brand-new person. How much less will our divine Parent, Jesus our Sibling, the Holy Spirit our Comforter, give up on you or me as we seek a closer communion with the Triune God?

The Jesus prayer comes from the Orthodox tradition. It originated around the fifth century as the simple repetition of the Savior's name and expanded over time to the phrase, "Lord Jesus Christ, Son of God, have mercy on me, a sinner." This simple phrase is meant to become what Orthodox Christians call a "prayer of the heart," or a prayer that, by grace, can fill your whole consciousness. Orthodox monastic communities grew up around the prayer, and laypersons of all classes adopted it too, as it can easily be prayed while doing other things: housework, traveling, walking. The nineteenth-century devotional classic *The Way of a Pilgrim* chronicles the adventures of an anonymous Russian peasant who roams the countryside praying the Jesus Prayer nonstop to obey Jesus's direction to "pray without ceasing."[5]

The Jesus prayer encapsulates much of Christian theology in just a few words, speaking truth about who God is and who we are in relation to God. Orthodox Bishop Kallistos Ware writes that the prayer "begins with adoration and ends with penitence." In offering it, we appeal to the One who is both human and divine to show us mercy, which we don't deserve but which it is God's nature to offer. The purpose of the Jesus prayer is not to leave us mired in misery over our sinfulness but to lead us into stillness where the Holy Spirit can turn us toward God's love and open us to it.

The words of the prayer draw our attention to Jesus, and it's intentionally repetitive. This repetition means that over the course of a period devoted to the prayer, our attention can move from the words themselves more and more fully to the person of Jesus and his love for us and the world. Some people, as they pray the Jesus prayer, start with the whole phrase and then slowly drop words to sharpen their focus.

Lord Jesus Christ, Son of God, have mercy on me, a sinner.
Lord Jesus Christ, Son of God, have mercy on me.
Lord Jesus Christ, Son of God, have mercy.
Lord Jesus Christ, Son of God.
Lord Jesus Christ.
Lord Jesus.
Jesus.

Generations of Orthodox Christians, and others who have learned from them, have found that, over time, praying the Jesus prayer can inform everything they do. Reading the news, for example, can become a different experience when we remember both our own need for penitence, which we share with all human beings, and the mercy God offers in Jesus Christ to all who ask his help to change our ways. What the Jesus prayer and centering prayer offer is the opportunity to create a space for stillness at our core: a stillness that can serve as both harbor and rudder as we navigate life's challenges.

To practice the Jesus prayer, set aside some time as you would for any prayer practice. As with centering prayer, consider setting a timer. Sit comfortably, close your eyes, and breathe deeply as you are able. Say slowly, "Lord Jesus Christ, Son of God, have mercy on me, a sinner." You can say the words out loud or silently; when starting out, it's advisable to say them aloud to improve your focus. Pause briefly (for one or two full inhalations and exhalations) after completing the phrase, and then say it again. Continue this way for the duration of your prayer time.

If you feel led to drop words off the prayer as sketched above, do that. If you feel led to fall silent altogether, you can do that too. If you find your mind wandering, take one or two cleansing breaths and then begin repeating the phrase. Don't critique or berate yourself or worry about getting the prayer wrong. The words aren't a magic spell that can go horribly awry if not said perfectly. They're a guidepost pointing to Jesus Christ's merciful love, and he will never spurn anyone who reaches out to him.

As you practice contemplative prayer, you may receive certain gifts: greater patience with yourself and others, a deeper sense of calm (or at least, more calm moments in your day), a stronger sense of God's presence, and a greater resolve to work for justice for God's beloved children who are persecuted. Another possible fruit of this practice is a deeper awareness of your own sin. This kind of awareness is rarely pleasant, but if it spurs you to confession and to accept God's forgiveness and grace to change your ways, it falls into the category of what Ignatius of Loyola called consolation: the movements of the Holy Spirit that draw us closer to God and make us better able to love our neighbors and ourselves as children of God.

Occasionally, contemplative prayers may offer more dramatic, obvious consolations. Once, while practicing centering prayer, I smelled roses in January when there were none anywhere near me; another time, I heard what seemed like God's voice saying, "Don't be afraid. I'm with you." (God is known for saying that.) Usually, though, centering prayer leaves me with a sense of peace or, sometimes, just slightly less anxiety than I carried into the session. Over time, these relatively small comforts have added up to a steady (but constant) sense of God's presence and a reliable practice of listening for the divine voice whether or not I'm consciously at prayer. For those gifts, I'm grateful.

Questions to consider and things to try

✛ Try either or both of the practices outlined in this chapter for a particular, pre-determined period of time: every day for a week or a couple of times a week for a month. After each session, write (or voice-record) some notes about what the practice was like, how you felt at the beginning and the end, and anything, in particular, you may have noticed (such as emotions that came and went or particularly intrusive thoughts). Try not to evaluate or critique yourself. Simply notice, and see if any patterns emerge.

✛ Ask a friend to join you in this practice, whether in the same room together, over videoconference, or separately. If you compare notes on your experiences, remember that each person is different. While a prayer practice may be a better fit for one person than another, it's not helpful to think of one person as being "better at" or "more successful with" a practice than another.

✛ After you have practiced centering prayer or the Jesus prayer for a little while, you may find yourself returning to them in spare moments. For example, if you arrive early for a medical appointment, you might stay outside the office for a few minutes to practice centering prayer; standing in line at the post office, you might offer the Jesus prayer silently for the length of time it takes you to reach the counter.

✛ If you usually pray the Daily Office or another highly verbal form of prayer and you find yourself tiring of it, consider practicing one of these forms of silent prayer or turning to one of the other non-verbal forms introduced in this book, for a week, a month, or from time to time. Listen for what God may say to you in the silence, or simply enjoy resting in God's quiet company.

Endnotes

[1] https://tractassociation.org/digital-material/meeting-for-worship/the-gathered-meeting, accessed 11 September 2020.

[2] 1 Kings 19:1-18.

[3] Contemplation is also a step in the practice of *lectio divina*, which I discuss in a separate chapter.

[4] Thomas Keating, OCSO, *Intimacy with God: An Introduction to Centering Prayer* (New York: The Crossroad Publishing Co., 2009).

[5] 1 Thessalonians 5:17.

[6] Kallistos Ware, *The Orthodox Way, Revised ed.* (Crestwood, NY: St. Vladimir's Seminary Press, 1995), 68. The bishop was born Timothy Ware, and some of his writing is published under that name.

Spiritual Direction

I have had an active practice of prayer for almost my whole adult life, and I still sometimes behave like Adam and Eve hiding in the garden or my friend Vernon Tyson's nervous parishioner that I mentioned in the introduction. I don't want to show God the nasty, petty side of myself: the grudges I nurse even though I know perfectly well I'm the only one they hurt or the impatience I show toward other drivers on the highway, even as I expect them to be gracious to me. I don't want God to know when I've run out of energy for the work to which I believe God once called me; I can't admit that the vocational path forward seems as invisible as in a blizzard white-out.

Consciously or unconsciously, I think, I can't tell God *that*.

And sometimes I forget God is waiting for me to show up and share what's on my mind, not impatiently drumming the divine fingers but with a smile. Sometimes I forget that God loves me just as I am: my need for repentance, my room for improvement, and all.

That's where my spiritual director comes in. To notice patterns in my thoughts or behavior that I'm too close to see; to kindly suggest that I might be tuning out the Spirit—or just plain lying to myself; and to encourage me by pointing to the ways in which I am faithful to Jesus's Way of love. My spiritual director is there to pass an hour each month praying with me about my life and to pray for me in between our meetings too.

My current director, Michael, has served in this role for more than a decade. In that time, he has seen me through personal crises, job changes, the deaths of friends and family members, the process of becoming a spiritual director myself, and the varied joys, challenges, and ordinary moments of everyday life. A member of the Society of Friends, he's one of four directors I've worked with; the others were an Episcopal priest, a Presbyterian pastor, and a Roman Catholic nun. In my experience, a director's insight, knack for compassionate truth-telling, and sense of humor are more important than their denominational affiliation. Above all, a director should be a person of frequent and honest prayer.

I found my first spiritual director when I was in my early thirties, a few months after being confirmed in the Episcopal Church. I knew I needed someone to hold me accountable to persist in prayer; someone to confess to when necessary; someone to help me listen for God's voice and to help me realize when the voice I was hearing or the impulse I was feeling was not of God. Spiritual direction was precisely the discipline I was looking for—and I call it a "discipline" on purpose. This practice is itself a form of prayer: time devoted, with another person, to being consciously in God's presence and listening for God's guidance. If asked, most directors will say that Jesus Christ, through the Holy Spirit, is the true director. The human director is present to listen to the Spirit with the directee. Session by session, they pay attention and reflect back what they notice, and in between sessions, the directee continues to pray and listen in light of their conversation. The goal of this practice is the same as any other Christian prayer discipline: to better love God, your neighbors, and yourself. And Christians have been seeking this kind of help from trusted siblings in faith for centuries.

✠ ✠ ✠

The twelfth-century Cistercian monk Aelred of Rievaulx wrote about what he called spiritual friendship: "You and I are here, and I hope that Christ is between us as a third. Now no one else is present to disturb the peace or to interrupt our friendly conversation."[1] Aelred's hope was grounded in Jesus's promise, recorded in Matthew 18, to be present wherever two or three of his disciples gathered in his name, and he offered his whole-hearted attention so that those he sat with might become more devoted friends to Christ.

For centuries, offering formal spiritual direction was considered the province of religious orders, especially men. Because directees might confess sins and require penance and absolution and because their thoughts might veer into heresy and require correction, the Roman Catholic Church long thought it most appropriate that priests (male by definition) serve as directors. Some nuns, however, served at least informally as directors to the sisters with whom they shared their lives and to women who visited convents for guidance. And there have always been people who were not formally ordained who lived more-or-less regular lives in the midst of their communities to whom others turned for spiritual conversation and counsel. Some may have been midwives or healers or guides in Indigenous traditions that co-existed with Christianity or simply neighbors with reputations as wise and attentive listeners.

A few were mystics, like fourteenth-century Julian of Norwich, who lived for decades enclosed in a cell attached to her English parish church, devoted to prayer and worship, listening for God's voice. Julian was no hermit: through a window that looked out from her cell onto a busy city street, she spoke with visitors seeking her guidance. Among them was Margery Kempe, a mystic from a town east of Norwich and another rare female author of the medieval period. Kempe, who was tried various times for heresy but never convicted, wrote later that the Lord had sent her to speak with Julian about her own conversations with God, "to find out if there were any deception in them, for the anchoress was expert in such things and could give good advice."[2]

Perhaps the best-known spiritual director, whose methods are still widely practiced half a millennium after he developed them, is Ignatius of Loyola, sixteenth-century founder of the Society of Jesus.[3] Behind his years of study and his development of the Spiritual Exercises and other methods of prayer was his overwhelming desire to "help souls," a phrase often repeated in his autobiography. Ignatius's approach to direction could be summed up as a program to teach Christians how to pay attention to their thoughts, feelings, and desires, depending on God for insight as they learned to, in the words of the New Testament, "test the spirits, to see whether they are from God."[4] Margery Kempe knew that not every thought and feeling that occurred to her in prayer arose from the Holy Spirit, and I know the same. That's why I rely on a director to listen with me.

People who are considering working with a spiritual director often wonder what makes it different from other relationships grounded in talking and listening, like therapy or an accountability group or partnership. As the name suggests, spiritual direction is explicitly spiritual, seeking to deepen the directee's relationship with God so they might better love God and their neighbor and grow more fully into who God created and calls them to be. Unlike therapists, spiritual directors are not trained to diagnose or treat mental illnesses. It can be extremely helpful to have done therapy before beginning spiritual direction, especially if you have experienced trauma or engage in unexamined patterns of destructive behavior, and therapy can help a person gain insight and perspective that will be helpful in spiritual direction. You can certainly work with both a spiritual director and a therapist in the same season of your life, but the focus in each relationship would be different. Spiritual direction is typically forward-looking, while therapy focuses on understanding the past to enable the patient or client to move into a healthier future.

Spiritual direction often explicitly returns the conversation to God, while therapy very well might not.

Here's an example. If a person experiences anxiety about money, even though they objectively have enough to live on and have no reason to fear destitution, a therapist might explore things like their family of origin's material circumstances, familial conflicts about money, and any complicated feelings the client might have about differences between their childhood and their current situation. A spiritual director might have a passing interest in those things and might ask whether the directee had already worked through those questions and feelings with a qualified therapist (and if they hadn't, the director might suggest they consider doing so). But a spiritual director would then be more likely to suggest that the directee contemplate some words of Jesus such as, "Consider the ravens: they neither sow nor reap, they have neither storehouse nor barn, and yet God feeds them. Of how much more value are you than the birds!"[5] Both the therapist and the director might help the person in question gain greater freedom from anxiety and openness to different ways of living. The spiritual director would have done so using resources of the Christian faith and focusing on accompanying the person as the Holy Spirit converts them more deeply to the Way of Jesus.

Spiritual direction also differs from an accountability group or partnership. That kind of relationship is designed to help Christians grow as disciples, praying, studying, giving, and living as the group members or partners agree they are called to. In that way, the intention is similar to spiritual direction. But there's an important difference. Accountability groups or partners are meant to be mutual relationships. A spiritual director, in contrast, is available to and focused on the directee in a way that is not mutual. The conversation that occurs in a spiritual direction session is not a back-and-forth of revelation, comfort, challenge, and assistance. Although the director may well find that the sessions give them insight into their own life and relationships, the two persons meet explicitly for the benefit of the directee—to help that particular soul, as Saint Ignatius would say. Unlike a mutual friendship, what Aelred called spiritual friendship happens within certain prescribed boundaries: the two parties get together at certain intervals (usually every four to six weeks); they typically do not meet outside those times; and the directee normally makes a financial offering for the director's time and attention.

✝ ✝ ✝

So, what actually happens in a spiritual direction session? And how might you know whether it would be a helpful practice for you?

Mostly, the directee talks and the director listens, which means this practice favors those who find it easy to talk about themselves. A director might ask a directee to devote the first session to sharing a brief spiritual autobiography, mentioning any high and low points, crossroads or moments of transformation, or persistent struggles, and saying something about how they typically pray. The directee should tell enough of their faith story and pertinent details about their current life to give the director a sense of who they are (for example, whether they're single or partnered, what kind of work they do, any avocations or hobbies they enjoy). More of the directee's story will come out over time, so there's no need to unspool the whole thread all at once.

In later sessions, the directee brings whatever's on their mind: a joy or struggle experienced in prayer, a conflict at work or home, some ongoing dilemma that needs a fresh perspective. Nothing, really, sits outside the scope of spiritual direction since God is present in all aspects of our lives, and we are called to love God with our whole selves. The director will listen, reflect on what they hear, and sometimes make suggestions about ways to pray or Bible passages to contemplate. They might say things like, "I wonder..." or ask, "Tell me more about what that feels like." They might refer to an image from scripture, like Jesus welcoming children or refusing to answer Pilate's questions, that affirms or challenges what the directee is offering. Each director's style is different, but their focus should always be on you and your relationship with God, however similar to or different from their own experience that might be.

If talking about yourself doesn't come easily to you, a director might invite you to share in more oblique ways: by talking about scriptural passages that resonate with you; by doodling, drawing, or writing in a prayerful way and then bringing something you have created to a session; by doing *lectio divina* in a session, or listening to music and reflecting on it. Over time, and as your relationship with the director deepens, you might find it becomes easier to share more directly about yourself.

If you're wondering whether working with a director might be right for you, here are some possible signs: You find yourself wanting to go deeper in your relationship with God or feel like you've hit a dry spell and need encouragement. You are entering a new stage of life, whether that's middle age, retirement, or graduating from university. You are considering making a substantial change (for example, switching jobs or careers) or may recently have gone through one (such as getting divorced). You have a vague feeling that something is missing, some change you might be called to make, but you don't have a clue what it is. You feel like a radio that's stuck between stations, picking up mostly static, and you want someone to help you tune out the noise and focus on receiving a clearer message. In any of these instances, working with a director might be helpful.

If you're ready to find a director, where might you start?

✢ Possible sources of referrals include:

> *Clergy or diocesan offices (Episcopal or Roman Catholic). During the coronavirus pandemic, many spiritual directors started working over the phone or by video conference, rather than seeing directees only in person. If you're comfortable with that medium, a wider pool of potential directors will be open to you, and you could seek referrals from fellow Christians in a wider variety of places.*

> *Professional associations like Spiritual Directors International (sdicompanions.org/) and Spiritual Directors of Color Network (sdcnetwork.org/). Because of structural racism in both society and the Church, most spiritual directors in North America are of European descent. The SDCN is an important resource both for directors of color, especially African Americans, and for people seeking such a director.*

✢ Once you have two or three possible names, make initial contact to ask for basic information about their approach, training, experience, and rates. Some directors may offer a sliding scale; it's not unreasonable to ask about that.

✢ Typically, a director will meet with you for a short, complimentary exploratory session of thirty to sixty minutes to give both of you an idea of whether you might work well together. In that session, the director would tell you something about themself and a bit more about how they do direction, and you would share something about why you are seeking it. The director should also cover the question of confidentiality; everything you say in a session should be completely confidential, except if you threaten to harm yourself or someone else. You might have this kind of exploratory session with one director or a few.

✜ When you and a director agree to work together, I recommend meeting three times (normally, for an hour every four to six weeks) as a trial period. Toward the end of the third session, the two of you would then discuss whether you feel led to continue the relationship. If not, you can find another director (and the current director may be able to offer a referral). If so, I recommend an intentional conversation annually to see if the relationship is still helpful to the directee, if anything about the practice needs to change, or if the relationship has served its purpose and can come to an end.

✜ This should go without saying, but unfortunately, it can't: you should feel physically and emotionally safe during every direction session. Your director's attention should be completely focused on you in ways that are appropriate to this kind of prayerful relationship. Any kind of sexual attention, or implicit or explicit prejudice about any aspect of your being (from race or gender to body type, and more), would be a reason to end the relationship immediately, to report your experience to anyone having authority over the director (such as their bishop or their Friends' Meeting), and possibly to take other appropriate legal or disciplinary action.

Endnotes

[1] Aelred of Rievaulx, *Spiritual Friendship*, trans. Lawrence C. Braceland and ed. Marsha Dutton, (Trappist, KY: Cistercian Publications, 2010), 55.

[2] Margery Kempe, *The Book of Margery Kempe*, trans. Barry Windeatt (New York: Penguin Classics, 2000), 77. The technical term for a woman who, like Julian, lives a life of prayer and contemplation confined to a cell, is "anchoress." The masculine form is "anchorite."

[3] I discuss his practices in the chapter on Ignatian prayer.

[4] 1 John 4:1.

[5] Luke 12:24.

Benediction

As this book draws to a close, I hold some hopes for you in my heart and in my prayers.

I hope this book has helped you in some way, maybe even in a way you didn't know you needed when you picked it up.

I hope you tried some of the practices discussed here.

I hope you haven't yet tried every single one, or if you have, I hope you gave yourself plenty of time in which to do so.

I hope you found a practice or two you enjoyed. If you found one or two you despised, I hope you realized that was just fine with God.

I hope you found a companion or two, or more, with and for whom to pray, who will pray for you, too.

I hope that, in those moments when you don't know how to pray, or when prayer seems pointless, you will remember what the Apostle Paul wrote more than two thousand years ago to the church in Rome: "[The] Spirit helps us in our weakness; for we do not know how to pray as we ought, but that very Spirit intercedes with sighs too deep for words" (Romans 8:26). It's still true.

I hope you will remember, always, that God loves you and deeply desires a closer relationship with you, and that because God is merciful and loving, you have nothing to fear from drawing near to God.

I hope you pass that good news on to someone else. I hope your prayers shape you—and my prayers shape me—into a disciple of Jesus whose life embodies something of his liberating, healing love. And I hope our prayers, together, help to reveal more and more of the resurrecting power of God on earth.

May all this, and more, be so. Amen.

Acknowledgments

I am grateful to say that in everything I do, I am blessed and helped by more people than I could count or name. Writing this book was no exception. And yet:

For Clarke, Kathy, and Kelly, who shared their experiences of prayer;

For Lauren, who read and improved every chapter;

For Richelle, Jason, and everyone on the Forward Movement staff;

For Ann and Jake, Catherine, Christine, Éric, Gwen, and Tammy and Holly, loving and encouraging friends;

and

For Wayne, who cheers me on daily, and our daughter, whose creativity inspires me;

I give particular thanks.

About the Author

Born and raised in Québec, the daughter of a francophone father and a Scottish immigrant mother, Rhonda Mawhood Lee moved to North Carolina to pursue a doctorate in history at Duke University. There, she found her life's companion and stayed. She has taught college and worked as an advocate for survivors of sexual assault and domestic violence and now serves as an Episcopal priest, writer, and spiritual director.

Lee's essays on faith and life have appeared in outlets like *America: The Jesuit Review, Faith & Leadership,* and *"Modern Love"* (The New York Times). She is the author of *Through with Kings and Armies: The Marriage of George and Jean Edwards* (Cascade Books, 2012). You can find her at rhondamawhoodlee.com.

About Forward Movement

Forward Movement is committed to inspiring disciples and empowering evangelists. Our ministry is lived out by creating resources such as books, small-group studies, apps, and conferences.

Our daily devotional, *Forward Day by Day*, is also available in Spanish (*Adelante Día a Día*) and Braille, online, as a podcast, and as an app for smartphones or tablets. It is mailed to more than fifty countries, and we donate nearly tens of thousands of copies each quarter to prisons, hospitals, and nursing homes.

We actively seek partners across the church and look for ways to provide resources that inspire and challenge. A ministry of the Episcopal Church for more than eighty years, Forward Movement is a nonprofit organization funded by sales of resources and by gifts from generous donors.

To learn more about Forward Movement and our resources, visit forwardmovement.org. We are delighted to be doing this work and invite your prayers and support.